Skills in English

Level 1

Listening

Terry Phillips

Garnet
EDUCATION

Published by
Garnet Publishing Ltd.
8 Southern Court
South Street
Reading RG1 4QS, UK

ISBN 1 85964 770 7

British Library Cataloguing-in-Publication Data
A catalogue record for this book is available from
the British Library.

Production

Project manager:	Richard Peacock
Editorial team:	Nicky Platt, Lucy Thompson, John Bates, Katharine Mendelsohn
Art director:	David Rose
Design:	Mark Slader
Illustration:	Beehive Illustration/Roger Wade Walker, Karen Rose, Ian West
Photography:	Corbis/Chris Lisle, Digital Vision, Flat Earth, Image Source, Photodisc

Garnet Publishing wishes to thank the following for their
assistance in the development of this project:
Dr Abdullah Al Khanbashi, Abderrazak Ben Hamida,
Maxine Gillway, Glenys Roberts and the Level 1 team at
UGRU, UAE University

Every effort has been made to trace the copyright holders
and we apologize in advance for any unintentional
omissions. We will be happy to insert the appropriate
acknowledgements in any subsequent editions.

Audio production: John Green TEFL Tapes

Printed and bound
in Lebanon by International Press

Skills in
English
Level 1
Listening

Contents

Book Map

Theme	Listening text type	Hearing consonants	Hearing vowels	Aural skills
1 Education, Student Life	Speech	/p/, /b/	Short vs long: /ɪ/ vs /iː/	• Understanding spoken definitions • Following instructions • Identifying names
2 Daily Life, Schedules	Lecture		Short vs long: /æ/ vs /ɑː/	• Understanding spoken times
3 Work and Business, Work Starts Now!	Lecture	/g/, /ʤ/		• Identifying important words • Predicting content
4 Science and Nature, So You Want to Be a Scientist?	Radio programme	/θ/, /ð/	Short vs long: /e/ vs /ɜː/	• Predicting the next word
5 The Physical World, Where Is Your Country?	Lecture	/s/, /z/	Short vs long: /ɒ/ vs /ɔː/	• Understanding spoken spellings
6 Culture and Civilization, Congratulations!	Student talk	/t/, /d/	Long: /uː/	• Understanding signpost language (1)
7 They Made Our World, Who? What? When?	Lecture	/ʃ/, /ʧ/		• Understanding signpost language (2) • Identifying dates
8 Art and Literature, There Was Once a Poor Man …	Radio programme		Diphthongs: /aɪ/, /eɪ/, /ɔɪ/	• Following a narrative
9 Sports and Leisure, Classifying Sports	Lecture		Diphthongs: /əʊ/, /aʊ/	• Recognising important words
10 Nutrition and Health, Nutrients and Food Groups	Lecture	Revision	Revision	• Revision

Introduction

THIS COURSE IS THE LISTENING COMPONENT of Level 1 of the *Skills in English* series. The series takes students in four levels from Elementary to Advanced level in the four skills, Listening, Speaking, Reading and Writing.

In addition, there is a remedial/false beginner course, *Starting Skills*, for students who are not ready to begin Level 1.

The listening component at each level is designed to build skills that help students survive in an academic institution where lectures are wholly or partly in English.

This component can be studied on its own or with one or more of the other components, e.g., Speaking and Reading.

The course is organised into themes, e.g., Science and Nature, Art and Literature. The same theme is used across the four skills. If, therefore, you are studying two or more components, the vocabulary and structures that you learn or practise in one component will be useful in another component.

Within each theme there are four lessons:

Lesson 1: *Vocabulary*
In the first lesson, you revise words from the theme that you have probably learnt already. You also learn some new words that you need to understand the texts in the rest of the theme.

Lesson 2: *Listening*
In this lesson, you practise skills that you have learnt in previous themes.

Lesson 3: *Learning new skills*
In this lesson, you learn one or more new skills to help you with listening.

Lesson 4: *Applying new skills*
In the final lesson, you use your new skills with another listening text. In most cases, the texts in Lessons 2 and 4 have a similar structure, so you can check that your skills have improved.

In this theme you are going to listen to some speeches to new students at a college.

Lesson 1: Vocabulary

You are going to learn some of the vocabulary you will need to understand the speeches.

A Discuss these questions in pairs. Use some of the red words.
1 What was your favourite subject at high school? Why did you like it?
2 Which subjects didn't you like? Why not?
3 Which is your best skill in English – listening, speaking, reading or writing? Which is your worst?

B 🔲 Listen to some sentences with the green words. Then complete each sentence with one of the words.
1 The _____ year in my country starts in October. All the students go back to high school then.
2 When does the second _____ start? Is it in February?
3 Which room is the _____ in? The one about learning English?
4 Mr Jones is in charge of the library. He is _____ for all the books and CD-ROMs.
5 Who is the _____ of Year 1? Is it Mrs Wright? Or is she in charge of Year 2?

C What is the connection between each pair of words? Match each pair to a connection.

1 history *and* mathematics	a) They are both places to study after you finish school.
2 principal *and* teacher	b) They are almost the same – one is British English and the other is American English.
3 college *and* university	c) They are both jobs in a school or college.
4 lecture *and* speech	d) They are both subjects.
5 term *and* semester	e) They both mean one person talking to a group of people.

D Find some more pairs of words in the red list. Explain the connection.

answer *(n and v)*
ask *(v)*
begin *(v)*
dictionary *(n)*
end *(v)*
explain *(v)*
history *(n)*
learn *(v)*
listen *(v)*
mathematics *(n)*
question *(n)*
read *(v)*
right *(adj)*
science *(n)*
spell *(v)*
student *(n)*
study *(v)*
teach *(v)*
test *(n and v)*
university *(n)*
write *(v)*
wrong *(adj)*
academic *(adj)*
college *(n)*
head *(n)*
in charge (of) *(adj)*
lecture *(n)*
principal *(n)*
responsible (for) *(adj)*
semester *(n)*
subject *(n)*
term *(n)*

Lesson 2: Listening

A Discuss the questions in pairs.

1 When did your academic year begin?
2 What is the name of the head of your college?
3 Who do you tell if you can't come to college one day?

B Look at a page from an information leaflet about Greenhill College. What information is missing? Make questions.

Example:

What is the surname of the principal?

C 🔊 It is the start of the college year at Greenhill College. The principal is welcoming the new students. Listen and add the missing information.

D Some words and phrases from the speech may be new to you. Match the words and their meanings.

1 principal   **a** information about the times of lectures
2 fees   **b** a teacher at a college or university
3 schedule   **c** the person in charge of a college
4 instructor   **d** money you pay to study
5 advisor   **e** a person who helps if you have problems

E 🔊 The principal explains the meaning of the words in Exercise D. Listen to his speech again and check your answers.

F Work in pairs. Make a sentence with each of the words in Exercise D. Then give a definition. Use one of the phrases from the Skills Check to introduce the definition.

Example:

How much are the fees – I mean the money you pay to study?

Greenhill College

Staff List

Name	Peter		Bill
		Penn	Beale
Title	Principal	Head of Year 1	
Room		23	16
Responsible for	fees		attendance

Skills Check

Waiting for definitions

When a person uses an unusual word in a speech or lecture, he or she often explains the meaning in the next few words.

Example:

*I'm the **principal** – that means I am **in charge of the whole place**.*

If you hear a word that is new to you, listen carefully. You may hear a definition. Listen for these phrases:

That means …   I mean …   In other words …   That is …

Lesson 3: Learning new skills

4 **A** 🔘 Listen and tick the words you hear. If you get three ticks in a line, say Bingo!

Card A

head	I mean	schedule
fees	principal	in charge of
instructor	attendance	advisor

Card B

fees ✓	advisor	principal ✓
head ✓	schedule ✓	I mean
instructor ✓	in charge of ✓	attendance

B Read Skills Check 1.

1 These words are from the speech in Lesson 2. Tick the correct column for the missing sound in each word.

words	p	b	words	p	b
… ay	✓		… lace		
… ill			… leased		
… enn			… eale		
… ersonal			… olly		
… ean			… rincipal		
… eter			… roblems		
… eo … le			… ehind		

5 **2** 🔘 Listen and check your answers.

6 **3** 🔘 Listen to these words connected with education. Is the missing letter *p* or *b*?

   a ___ook **d** s___ell **g** su___ject
   b pa___er **e** ___ass **h** ex___lain
   c ___egin **f** ___eriod

C Read Skills Check 2.

1 Study these examples.

fill	feel
hill	pleased
is	means
this	see
will	me
give	she's
his	he's
if	we

Skills Check 1

Hearing consonants – *p* and *b*

These two sounds in English are very similar but they make different words. Make sure you can hear the difference.

Example: *pen / Ben*

Skills Check 2

Hearing vowels – *fill* and *feel*

These two sounds in English are very similar but they make different words. Make sure you can hear the difference. The sound in *feel* is longer.

7 **2** 🔘 Look at these pairs of words. Listen. Which do you hear in each case? Don't worry about the meanings.

a hill ✓	heal		**f** kill ✓	keel	
b still	steal ✓		**g** fill	feel ✓	
c will ✓	wheel		**h** fit	feet ✓	
d mill	meal ✓		**i** Bill ✓	Beale	
e pill ✓	peel		**j** bit	beat ✓	

3 How can you spell the short sound? What about the longer sound?

D 🔘 Listen to the first part of the principal's speech again. It's much slower this time. Put your left hand up every time you hear *p*. Put your right hand up every time you hear *b*.

E 🔘 Listen to the second part of the speech again. Say *i* every time you hear the short sound. Say *ee* every time you hear the long sound.

Lesson 4: Applying new skills

1	Sat	Sun	Mon	Tue	Wed
Morning	English	English	English	English	English
.	Lunch	Lunch	Lunch	Lunch	Lunch
Afternoon	General Studies	General Studies	General Studies	General Studies	General Studies

2	Sat	Sun	Mon	Tue	Wed
Morning	General Studies	General Studies	General Studies	General Studies	General Studies
	Lunch	Lunch	Lunch	Lunch	Lunch
Afternoon	English	English	English	English	English

3	Sat	Sun	Mon	Tue	Wed
Morning	English	Maths	English	Maths	English
	Lunch	Lunch	Lunch	Lunch	Lunch
Afternoon	General Studies	General Studies	Maths	General Studies	General Studies

Ⓐ Find on this page:
- three subjects
- five days
- two periods of time
- five surnames
- five numbers
- three schedules
- one staff list

Ⓑ 〇〇 Listen to some sentences from the principal's speech in Lesson 2. What is Mrs Penn going to talk about? Tick (✔) one or more topic.

___ lectures   ___ responsibilities
___ meetings   ___ instructors
___ personal advisors   ___ the schedule

Ⓒ 〇〇 Listen to Mrs Penn's speech. <u>Underline</u> the topics to check your answers to Exercise B.

Ⓓ Imagine you are a new student at Greenhill College.
  1 〇〇 Listen to the first part of Mrs Penn's speech again. Which schedule above is correct for you?
  2 〇〇 Listen to the second part of Mrs Penn's speech again. What is the name of your personal advisor? Tick one.

Ⓔ Read Mrs Penn's speech on page 52. Check your answers to Exercise D.

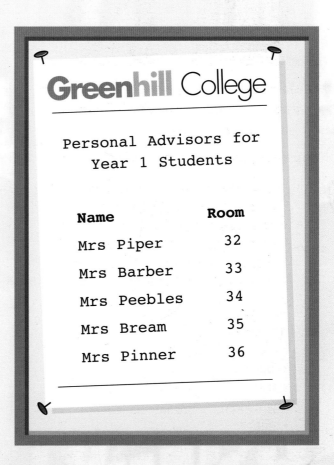

Greenhill College

Personal Advisors for Year 1 Students

Name	Room
Mrs Piper	32
Mrs Barber	33
Mrs Peebles	34
Mrs Bream	35
Mrs Pinner	36

afternoon *(n)*
autumn *(n)*
day *(n)*
evening *(n)*
first *(adj)*
hour *(n)*
last *(adj)*
late *(adj)*
later *(adj)*
midnight *(n)*
minute *(n)*
month *(n)*
morning *(n)*
night *(n)*
noon *(n)*
now *(adv)*
o'clock *(adv)*
past *(adv and n)*
quarter *(n)*
spring *(n)*
summer *(n)*
time *(n)*
today *(n)*
tomorrow *(n)*
tonight *(n)*
week *(n)*
winter *(n)*
year *(n)*
yesterday *(n)*
campus *(n)* ____
chess *(n)* ____
club *(n)* ____
film *(n)* ____
music *(n)* ____
plan *(v)*
restaurant *(n)* ①
sports *(n)* ____

In this theme you are going to listen to a talk about schedules. You're also going to hear some information about things to do after college work each day.

Lesson 1: Vocabulary

You are going to learn some of the vocabulary you will need to understand the talk.

A Discuss these questions in pairs. They use some of the red words.
  1 What are you doing this evening?
  2 What about tomorrow morning?
  3 Have you got any plans for next week?
  4 What do you usually do on Thursday and Friday?
  5 Do you do different things in the evening in the summer and the winter?

B Find the opposite of each word below in the list of red words.
  1 morning
  2 day
  3 midnight
  4 first
  5 yesterday
  6 summer

C 🎧 Listen to some sentences with the green words. Number the words in order.
  Example:
  1 There is a very good **restaurant** in North Road. The food is excellent.

Lesson 2: Listening

(A) Discuss these questions in pairs.

1 How many classes do you have each day?
2 Do you have the same number of classes every day?
3 What time does the first class start?
4 What time does the last class end?
5 Do you have a break for lunch?

9.00	Days	Ends
10.00		General
Studies		Monday
Times		

(B) Here is a planner in which students can write their schedules. Complete the planner by writing in the missing information from the yellow box.

			Saturday	Sunday		Tuesday	Wednesday	Thursday
Period	**Begins**							
1								
2								
3								
Lunch								
4								
5								
6								

(C) Students at Greenhill College have to fill in their schedules. Mrs Penn, the head of Year 1, gives the information. She uses the words in the blue box.

1 What does each word mean? Use some of the words from the yellow box in each definition.
2 🔊 Listen to Mrs Penn's definitions and check your answers.

| schedule recess |
| period cafeteria |

| between break campus classes |
| days part restaurant short times |

(D) 🔊 Mrs Penn is going to give you your schedule. Listen and answer these questions.

1 What time does the first lesson start? *9*
2 How long is each lesson? *1hr*
3 How long is the break between each lesson? *10m*
4 How long is the lunch break? *1hr*

(E) 🔊 Listen again.

1 Check your answers to the questions in D.
2 Fill in the dark green columns of the planner.

Revision

(F) The words in the table are from the talk.

1 Put a tick in the correct column, according to the sound.
2 🔊 Listen and check your ideas.

(G) The words below are from the talk.

1 Is the missing letter *b* or *p*?
2 🔊 Listen and check your ideas.

a a___out
b ___ecause
c ___egins
d ___encil
e ___etween
f ___reak
g s___ace
h cam___us
i ___art
j ___eriod

		1	2
		fill	feel
		/ɪ/	/iː/
a	each		
b	give		
c	mean		
d	read		
e	see		
f	six		
g	this		
h	three		
i	begins		
j	between		

Lesson 3: Learning new skills

A Think of a word for each definition. Find the hidden word that connects them all.

1	the days and times of classes	
2	it helps to organise your day/week/month/year	
3	all the buildings of the college	
4	the restaurant on the campus	
5	a short break between classes	
6	the day before Sunday	
7	the day after Tuesday	
8	a part of the college day	

B Can you understand spoken times in English?

1 🔘 Listen to eight times. Letter the clocks A to H.

2 Study Skills Check 1.

3 🔘 Listen to the times again and check.

4 Number the clocks in order (earliest = 1).

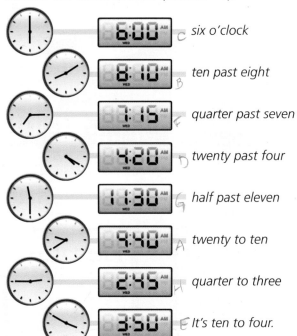

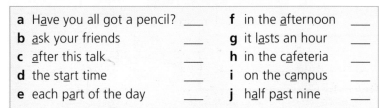

six o'clock — *C*
ten past eight — *B*
quarter past seven — *F*
twenty past four — *D*
half past eleven — *G*
twenty to ten — *A*
quarter to three — *H*
It's ten to four. — *E*

Skills Check 1

Understanding spoken times

Study the clocks and the words.

It's ...

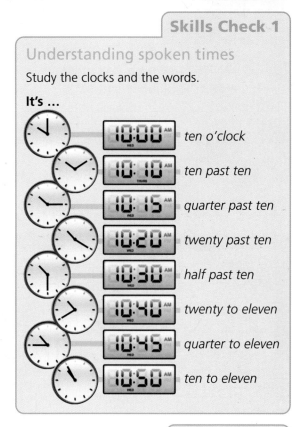

ten o'clock
ten past ten
quarter past ten
twenty past ten
half past ten
twenty to eleven
quarter to eleven
ten to eleven

C Look at the phrases in the blue box. They are all from the talk in Lesson 2.

1 How do you say each underlined vowel <u>a</u>?

2 Read Skills Check 2. Write S (short) or L (long) for each underlined vowel.

3 🔘 Listen and check your ideas.

a	H<u>a</u>ve you all got a pencil? ___	**f**	in the <u>a</u>fternoon ___
b	<u>a</u>sk your friends ___	**g**	it l<u>a</u>sts an hour ___
c	<u>a</u>fter this talk ___	**h**	in the c<u>a</u>feteria ___
d	the st<u>a</u>rt time ___	**i**	on the c<u>a</u>mpus ___
e	each p<u>a</u>rt of the day ___	**j**	h<u>a</u>lf p<u>a</u>st nine ___

Skills Check 2

Hearing vowels – /æ/ and /ɑː/

The vowel *a* has two common sounds:

1 the short sound in *have*   /hæv/

2 the long sound in *half*   /hɑːf/

You must hear the difference.

Note: The vowel *a* can make other sounds, too.

*a*ll = /ɔː/

a pencil = /ə/

d*ay* = /eɪ/

etc.

Lesson 4: Applying new skills

A Two words are similar. One is different. Circle the odd one out. Write the letter of the reason.

1 schedule	timetable	semester	**a**	It is not a day of the week.
2 cafeteria	recess	restaurant	**b**	It is not a list of days, times and classes.
3 March	Wednesday	Monday	**c**	It is not a place to eat.
4 period	class	planner	**d**	It is not a subject.
5 recess	schedule	break	**e**	It is not a time between classes.
6 General Studies	English	Friday	**f**	It is not part of the college day.

B Discuss these questions in pairs.
1 What do you do after college each day?
2 What clubs do you go to?
3 Why do you go to those clubs?

C 🔊 Mrs Penn runs the extracurricular activities at Greenhill College. Listen and find out:
1 the meaning of *extracurricular*.
2 the extracurricular activities at the college – tick the activities on the notice board.

D 🔊 Listen again and write in the days and times for each activity that you ticked.

E Read the talk on page 54. Check your answers to Exercise D.

F Which of the clubs would you join? Why?

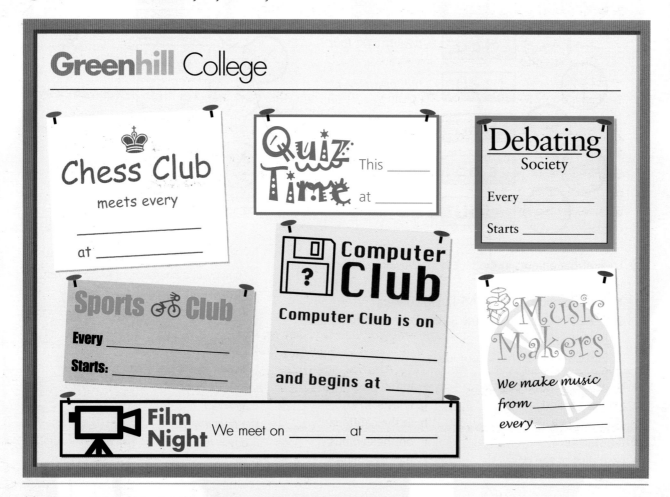

In this theme you are going to listen to a talk about work.

Lesson 1: Vocabulary

You are going to learn some of the vocabulary you will need to understand the talk.

(A) Discuss these questions in pairs. Use some of the red words.

1 Have you ever had a job? What was it? Did you like it? Why (not)?

2 What sort of job would you like when you leave college?

3 What sort of job would you hate? Why?

(B) 🔊 Listen to some sentences with the green words. Then complete each sentence.

1 People don't like him at work. They can't _____ him. They never know if he will be late, or not come to work at all.

2 It is very important to have good _____ to work with in a job.

3 That work isn't _____. You can do it tomorrow.

4 Where are the _____ for my next meeting? Are they in the file?

5 If you are paid every month, we call that money your _____.

6 Some companies make _____ – real things like computers, televisions or cars.

7 Some companies give _____ – like banks, cleaning companies or car hire companies.

(C) What is the connection between each pair of words? Match each pair to a connection.

1 products *and* services   **a** Companies make or give them.

2 factories *and* offices   **b** They are both people at work.

3 files *and* papers   **c** They are both places of work.

4 managers *and* colleagues   **d** You put one in the other.

(D) Find some more pairs of words in the red list. Explain the connection.

---

company *(n)*

computer *(n)*

desk *(n)*

e-mail *(n)*

envelope *(n)*

factory *(n)*

file *(n)*

job *(n)*

letter *(n)*

manager *(n)*

office *(n)*

secretary *(n)*

shelf / shelves *(n)*

shop *(n)*

start *(v)*

supermarket *(n)*

typist *(n)*

website *(n)*

work *(n and v)*

working hours *(n)*

colleague *(n)*

papers *(n)*

product *(n)*

rely on *(v)*

salary *(n)*

service *(n)*

urgent *(adj)*

Lesson 2: Listening

A Discuss these questions in pairs.
1 What are the most important things to do when you have a job?
2 What are the main differences between having a job and going to college?
3 What are the main similarities between the two?

Track 26 **B** 🔊 Gerald Gardiner is a management consultant. He is at Greenhill College today. He is talking to the first-year students about work. Listen to the first part of his talk.
1 How many points does he make?
2 Can you remember any of the points?

Track 27 **C** 🔊 Listen again. How does he define these words? Match each word to a definition.

1 punctual	**a** desk, shelves, cupboards
2 manager	**b** good or bad
3 colleagues	**c** always on time
4 customers	**d** ordered by date
5 tasks	**e** pieces of work
6 quality	**f** the people who buy things from your company
7 workplace	**g** the people you work with
8 chronologically	**h** the person who gives you orders

D Complete these notes from the talk with a verb in each space.

Track 28 **E** 🔊 Listen again and check your answers.

Revision

F The words below are from the talk.
1 Put a tick in the correct column, according to the underlined sound.

Track 29 2 🔊 Listen and check your ideas.

	A	B	C	D
	fill	feel	have	half
	/ɪ/	/iː/	/æ/	/ɑː/
<u>a</u>re				✓
b<u>a</u>d			✓	
coll<u>ea</u>gues				
g<u>i</u>ves				
k<u>ee</u>p				
l<u>ea</u>ve				
m<u>a</u>nager				
p<u>eo</u>ple				
p<u>ie</u>ces				
st<u>a</u>rt				
th<u>a</u>t				
th<u>i</u>nk				

You must:
1 _____ to work every day
2 __be__ punctual
3 __respect your__ manager / colleagues
   also
4 __respect__ customers
5 __do__ all tasks
6 __complete__ all tasks on time
7 __be__ responsible for quality of work
8 __keep your__ workplace tidy
9 __organise__ work files sensibly

G The words below are from the talk.
1 What is the missing letter in each case?

a __p__unctual	**g** jo__b__
b res__p__ect	**h** com__p__any
c __b__uy	**i** res__p__onsible
d __p__ieces	**j** work__p__lace
e sensi__b__ly	**k** com__p__lete
f __p__eople	**l** __p__erson

2 🔊 Listen and check your ideas.

Lesson 3: Learning new skills

A Think of a word to complete each sentence. Find the hidden phrase that connects them all.

1 You must be ..., in other words, on time.	P	U	N	C	T	U	A	L							
2 You must ... things – put them in order.					O	R	G	A	N	I	S	E			
3 Work with your ..., the people who study with you.	C	O	L	L	E	A	G	U	E	S					
4 Your work must be good	Q	U	A	L	I	T	Y								
5 Keep your ... in order.	F	I	L	E	S										
6 Your instructor is your ... at college.	M	A	N	A	G	E	R								
7 You must ... people, especially your instructors.	R	E	S	P	E	C	T								
8 You must keep your ... tidy.				W	O	R	K	P	L	A	C	E			
9 Think of college as a				J	O	B									
10 You are ... for your own work – if it's good, or bad.				R	E	S	P	O	N	S	I	B	L	E	
11 Do all your ... well and on time.	T	A	S	K	S										

B Read Skills Check 1.

1 Find and underline the important words in these sentences from the talk in Lesson 2.

  a You must <u>go</u> to work <u>every day</u>.

  b You must be <u>punctual</u>.

  c You must <u>respect</u> your <u>manager</u> and your <u>colleagues</u>.

  d You must also <u>respect</u> the <u>customers</u>.

  e You must do <u>all</u> the <u>tasks</u> or pieces of work that your manager gives you.

  f You must <u>complete</u> all your tasks on <u>time</u>.

  g You are <u>responsible</u> for the <u>quality</u> of your work.

  h You must <u>keep</u> your <u>workplace</u> tidy.

  i You must <u>organise</u> your work files <u>sensibly</u>.

Track 31 **2** 📼 Listen and check your ideas.

C Read Skills Check 2.

1 Write these words from the talk in the correct place, according to the sound of *g*:

  go give college get change colleague organise

2 📼 Listen and check your answers.

3 Now put these words into the correct place:

  age page begin charge ago again large big

33 **4** 📼 Listen and check your answers.

5 What about these words?

  danger angry wage magazine rig

6 📼 Listen and check your answers.

A	*good /g/*	go
B	*manager /dʒ/*	college

> ### Skills Check 1
>
> #### Hearing important words
>
> When a speaker gets to an important word in a sentence, he or she often says it **more loudly**. Listen for the loud words in each sentence. These are the important words for you to write down.
> **Examples:**
>
> | You hear... | You write ... |
> |---|---|
> | You must **go** to work **every day**. | *go every day* |
> | You must be **punctual**. | *punctual* |
> | You must **respect** your **manager** and your **colleagues**. | *respect manager + colleagues* |

> ### Skills Check 2
>
> #### Hearing consonants – g
>
> The consonant *g* has two common sounds:
> **1** The sound in *good, go*.
> **2** The sound in *college, manager*.

Lesson 4: Applying new skills

(A) Find pairs of words or phrases in the yellow box. Explain the connection.
Example: alphabetical and chronological = They are two ways of organising information.

> alphabetical buy chronological colleague customers in order job manager on time organise punctual task

(B) Gerald Gardiner says (Lesson 2) that there are nine things you must do in a job.
1 How many can you remember? Just say important words.
Examples: *go every day, punctual*
2 Look at the first column of the blue table and check your ideas.

Skills Check
Predicting content

You should always think: *What is the speaker going to say next?* Then listen and check your ideas. Predicting will help you to listen with understanding.

(C) Why must you do each thing in column 1 of the blue table? Think of a good reason. Make some notes in the *Our reasons* column.

(D) Gerald gives a reason for each action in the second part of his talk.

CD2 – T1
1 🔘 Listen and write one or two stressed words under *Gerald's reasons* in the blue table. Guess the spelling.
2 🔘 Listen again. Are Gerald's reasons the same as yours?

(E) Work in groups. Look at the list of things you must do in a job (in the blue table). What about college? Must you do the same sort of things to be successful?

You must ...	Our reasons	Gerald's reasons
go every day		rely
be punctual		expect you
respect your manager and your colleagues		well together
respect the customers		pay wages
do all the tasks that your manager gives you		boring tasks
complete all your tasks on time		need information
be responsible for the quality of your work		dissatisfied
keep your workplace tidy		made mess
organise your work files sensibly		

In this theme you are going to listen to a talk about science as a career and the scientific method.

Lesson 1: Vocabulary

You are going to learn some of the vocabulary you will need to understand the talk.

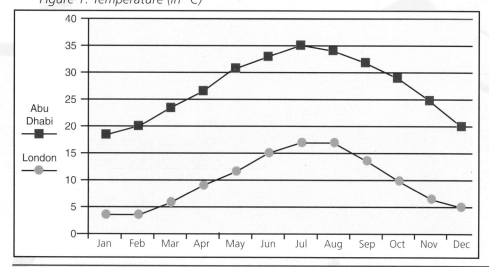

Ⓐ Find in the red words:

1 nine colours
2 seven natural features
3 five weather conditions

Ⓑ Match the red words and the colours.

1 grass   **a** blue or grey
2 cloud   **b** brown and green
3 sun   **c** green
4 sky   **d** red, yellow or orange
5 flower   **e** red, yellow, orange, white or blue
6 snow   **f** white
7 tree   **g** white, grey or black

Ⓒ 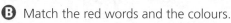 Listen to a paragraph. Then write one of the green words in each space.

_____ is the study of how things work in the world. A _____ usually works in a _____. He or she _____ things to find out the facts. He or she often puts the facts in a _____, with columns of information, or in a _____, with blocks or lines that represent the information.

Table 1: Temperatures (in °C)

	Jan	Feb	Mar	Apr	May	Jun	Jul	Aug	Sep	Oct	Nov	Dec
Abu Dhabi	19	20	23	27	31	33	35	34	32	29	25	20
London	4	4	6	9	12	15	17	17	14	10	7	5

Figure 1: Temperature (in °C)

Red words:

black *(adj)*
blue *(adj)*
brown *(adj)*
cold *(adj)*
colour *(n and v)*
cloud *(n)*
flower *(n)*
fog *(n)*
forest *(n)*
grass *(n)*
green *(adj)*
grey *(adj)*
hot *(adj)*
island *(n)*
lake *(n)*
mountain *(n)*
orange *(adj)*
rain *(n and v)*
red *(adj)*
river *(n)*
sea *(n)*
sky *(n)*
snow *(n and v)*
sun *(n)*
temperature *(n)*
thunderstorm *(n)*
tree *(n)*
water *(n)*
weather *(n)*
white *(adj)*
wind *(n)*
yellow *(adj)*

Green words:

graph *(n)*
laboratory *(n)*
science *(n)*
scientific *(adj)*
scientist *(n)*
table *(n)*
test *(v)*

Lesson 2: Listening

A Discuss the questions in pairs.
1 What do you think of when you hear the word *science*?
2 Are you interested in science?
3 Would you like to be a scientist?

B Look at the information on the right. It is about a radio programme. Then work in pairs to discuss these questions.
1 Where can you see information like this?
2 What time does the programme start?
3 What is the programme about?
4 Who is the programme for?

C Arthur is going to talk about four points.
1 🔘 Listen to the introduction to the programme. Tick (✓) each point in the programme information when Arthur mentions it.
2 🔘 Listen to the first part of the programme. Put your hand up when Arthur starts to talk about a new point.

D 🔘 Listen again. How does Arthur Burns define these words?
1	proving	**a**	a test in a laboratory
2	method	**b**	looking up information, e.g., in a library
3	hypothesis	**c**	an idea of the truth
4	experiment	**d**	information before it is organised
5	research	**e**	a way of doing something
6	data	**f**	what you learn from an experiment
7	conclusions	**g**	showing that something is always true

E 🔘 Look at the student notes on the right. Listen to the first part of the programme again. Complete the notes by writing one word in each space.

Revision

F The words below are from the talk.
1 Tick the correct column, according to the underlined sound.
2 🔘 Listen and check your ideas.

	A fill /ɪ/	B feel /iː/	C have /æ/	D half /ɑː/
d<u>i</u>splay	✓			
<u>e</u>ven		✓		
<u>e</u>nough				
gr<u>a</u>ph				
Gr<u>ee</u>k				
h<u>a</u>ppen				
<u>i</u>f				
l<u>a</u>b				
p<u>a</u>st				
pl<u>a</u>nt				

9.15 So you want to be …
a scientist?

In this week's programme, Arthur Burns looks at science as a career.
• What is science?
• What do scientists do?
• What is *scientific method?*
• Is science the right career for you?

~~9.45 The World in View~~

Science = Greek / Latin to
_____
Science = Knowing things +
_____ things
Scientific method:
_____ a hypothesis.
_____ the hypothesis.
_____ an experiment
or _____ some research.
_____ data.
_____ the results in a table
or a graph.
_____ conclusions.
_____ or disprove the
hypothesis.

G The words below are from the programme.
1 What are the missing letters?
2 🔘 Listen and check your ideas.
a	____rove	**f**	dis____rove
b	dis____lay	**g**	hy____othesis
c	____oth	**h**	ex____eriment
d	ta____le	**i**	la____
e	____ast	**j**	ha____ ____en

Lesson 3: Learning new skills

A Think of a word to complete each sentence. Find the hidden word that connects them all.

1 ... is looking up information, e.g. in a library.	
2 You can draw ... from a good 3.	
3 You do these in a laboratory.	
4 A ... is a way of doing something.	
5 I think it's true, but I don't ...	
6 A ... is an idea of the truth about something.	
7 Scientists use ... method.	
8 We often put these in a table or on a graph.	
9 This is information before it is organised.	

B Read Skills Check 1. Answer the questions.
  1 What is it about?
  2 Why should you try to predict the next word?

C You are going to hear some parts of the radio programme in Lesson 2 again.
  1 Look at the words in the yellow box. Think of sentences from the radio programme with these words.
  2 📼 Listen to some of Arthur's sentences. Choose the next word from the yellow box each time Arthur pauses. Write the number beside the word.

data	graph	know	method	true	world

D Read Skills Check 2.
  1 Put these words from the talk into the correct column, according to the sound of *th*.
    that the they both then there hypothesis with thing truth
  2 📼 Listen and check your answers.

A	B
think	this
/θ/	/ð/

E Answer the questions.
  1 Which is the odd one out?
    test when then pen she bed many any head again
  2 📼 Listen and check your answers.
  3 Work in pairs. What do all these words have in common?
    bird first heard learn person research surname turn work world
  4 Read Skills Check 3. Did you get the right answer to Exercise 3?

Skills Check 1

What comes next?

We can often predict the next word in a talk. **Examples:** *Science is about knowing things, but even more it is about proving ...* **things.**
I know that plants need sunlight to live. At least, I think that's ... **true.**
They can do research, which means looking up ... **information.**
If you can predict the next word, you can listen with more understanding.

Skills Check 2

Hearing consonants – th

The consonants *th* have two sounds:
1 The soft sound in *think, thing.*
2 The harder sound in *this, that, the.*

Skills Check 3

Hearing vowels – e or er?

The vowel sound in *then* is usually written with *e*. But there are some common words with *a* or *ea*:
Examples: *many, any, head*
The vowel sound in *her* is written in many different ways: *res**ear**ch, w**or**d, b**ir**d, t**ur**n.*
In AmE, we can hear the *r* sound in these words.

Lesson 4: Applying new skills

A Match the verb with the end of the sentence to describe the scientific method.

1	Make	**a**	an experiment or some research
2	Test	**b**	conclusions
3	Do	**c**	data
4	Collect	**d**	the hypothesis, or disprove it
5	Display	**e**	the hypothesis
6	Draw	**f**	the results in a table or a graph
7	Prove	**g**	a hypothesis

B ▢ Listen to the next part of the programme with Arthur Burns. What does Arthur ask you to do? Make a sentence with these groups of words.

an experiment   and water   plants need sunlight   Think of   to live   to prove that

C Work in groups. Think of an experiment to prove that plants need sunlight and water.

D ▢ Listen to the next part of the programme. When Arthur stops speaking, say the next word.

E Complete this description of the experiment with a suitable word in each space.

1 I bought three plants of the same _____.
2 I put each plant into a pot which was the same _____.
3 I filled each pot with the same kind of _____.
4 I put each plant pot on a _____.
5 I put all three plants _____.
6 I covered Plant 1 with black _____.
7 I watered Plant 1 and Plant 3 for one _____.
8 I did not give Plant 2 any _____.
9 What result did I _____?
10 Remember: Plant 1 did not have any _____.
11 It was yellow and very _____.
12 Plant 2 did not have any _____.
13 It was _____.
14 Plant 3 had sunlight and _____.
15 It was green and _____.

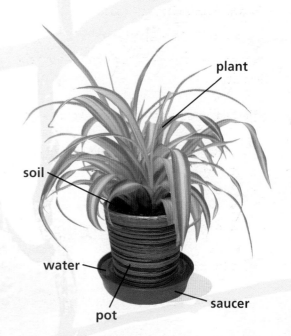

plant

soil

water

saucer

pot

F Read the talk on page 56. Check your answers to Exercise E.

G Do you think a career in science is right for you? Why (not)?

In this theme you are going to listen to a lecture about a country – its location and physical features.

Lesson 1: Vocabulary

You are going to learn some of the vocabulary you will need to understand the lecture.

A Make true sentences about your country. Use some of the red words.

B Look at the map of the world. Which countries are:
1 north of the Equator?
2 south of the Equator?
3 on the Tropic of Cancer?
4 on the Tropic of Capricorn?

C Listen to descriptions of six countries. Look at the map. Find each country.

D Where is your country? Look at the world map. Describe the location.

E Look at the diagram. Country A has a border with Country B, Country C and Country D. Which countries does your country have a border with?

Country B	Country A	Country D
	Country C	

behind (prep)
between (prep)
corner (n)
country (n)
east (n)
in front of (prep)
in the centre of (prep)
left (n)
near (prep)
next to (prep)
north (n)
opposite (prep)
south (n)
town (n)
west (n)
border (n and v)
continent (n)
locate (v)
location (n)
the Equator (n)
the Tropic of Cancer (n)
the Tropic of Capricorn (n)

Lesson 2: Listening

A Discuss these questions in pairs.
1 Which country do you come from?
2 Where is your country?
3 What's your hometown / city?
4 Which part of your country is that in?

B Donna, Fatma and Fairuza are students at Greenhill College. They are talking before a lecture.
1  Listen. Donna pauses a few times in her questions. Guess the word she is going to say next on each occasion. Listen and check your ideas.
2 Complete the blue table.
3 Listen again. Complete the information about Kuwait and Oman.

C The three girls are majoring in Geography. The title of the lecture today is:

> THE SULTANATE OF OMAN
> LOCATION AND PHYSICAL FEATURES

What information do you expect to hear in the lecture?
1 Make a list in groups.
2 Keep your list safely. You will need it for Lesson 4.

Revision

D The words below are from the conversation.
1 Tick in the correct column, according to the underlined vowel sound(s).
2 Listen and check your ideas.

	A	B	C	D	E
	fill	feel	have	half	head
	/ɪ/	/iː/	/æ/	/ɑː/	/e/
ci<u>t</u>y					
d<u>i</u>d					
<u>ea</u>st					
<u>exa</u>ctly					
Om<u>a</u>n					
s<u>ai</u>d					
Sal<u>a</u>lah					
sp<u>e</u>ll					
w<u>e</u>st					

The country is in the _____ of the Gulf. It is north-_____ of Saudi Arabia, south of Iraq and west of Iran. The _____ is Kuwait City.

The _____ is on the Arabian Sea. It is _____-east of the UAE and Saudi Arabia. The _____ is Muscat.

Student	Country	Hometown
Fatma		
Fairuza		

E The words below are from the conversation.
1 Complete each word with one or two letters.
2 Listen and check your ideas.
a a___out   d ___art
b ca___ital   e sou____
c nor____   f s___ell

F Listen and complete these words from earlier themes.
1 colle___e   6 me____od
2 dis___lay   7 ___ast
3 ex___eriment   8 ___rove
4 ___ob   9 ___ink
5 mana___er   10 ___unctual

Lesson 3: Learning new skills

A Solve the crossword.

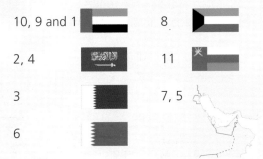

10, 9 and 1

8

2, 4

11

3

7, 5

6

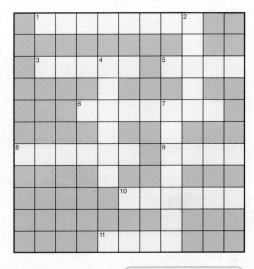

B Read Skills Check 1.

1 Say the example words.

2 Say the letter above each word.

3 🔊 Listen and put the other letters of the alphabet into the correct column, according to the vowel sound.

A	B	F	Q	I	O	R
.						

C 🔊 Listen to the spellings on the cassette.

1 Write the letters and find out the names of the countries.

2 Check your answers in pairs.

D Read Skills Check 2.

1 What are the two sounds of *s*?

2 What is the sound of *s* in each of these words from the conversation in Lesson 1?

it's   is   small   south   has   east   coast
what's   sorry   does   spell   say   towns

3 🔊 Listen and check your ideas.

E Work in pairs.

1 Which is the odd one out?

on   not   from   what   come   of
sorry   want   was   wash

2 What do all these words have in common?

for   before   more   small   talk   war
August   taught   north

3 Read Skills Check 3. Did you get the right answers to Exercises 1 and 2?

4 🔊 Listen to the words in Exercises 1 and 2.

Skills Check 1

Understanding spoken spellings

Speakers sometimes spell out important words.

Fairuza: I'm from Salalah.
Donna: *How do you spell that?*
Fairuza: S-A-L-A-L-A-H.

You must be able to hear the names of letters correctly. There are seven vowel sounds.

Sounds

A	B	F	Q	I	O	R
wage	*three*	*ten*	*you*	*time*	*no*	*are*

Skills Check 2

Hearing consonants – *s*

The consonant *s* can have two sounds:
1 The sound at the beginning of *s*ounds.
2 The sound at the end of *sound*s.

Skills Check 3

Hearing vowels – *o* / *or*

1 The vowel sound in *not* is usually written with *o*.
Examples: *on, from, sorry*
But there are some common words with *a*.
Examples: *want, what, was, wash*

2 The vowel sound in *north* is usually written with *or(e)*.
Examples: *for, before, more*
But there are some common words with *al, ar, aw* or *au*.
Examples: *small, talk, war, August, draw*

Lesson 4: Applying new skills

A Which is the odd one out in each set of letters?
Explain your answer.

1 A H J O   3 F V M N
2 B C R D   4 Q U W Y

B You are going to hear the first part of this lecture:

> THE SULTANATE OF OMAN
> LOCATION AND PHYSICAL FEATURES

1 Look at the list of points you made for Lesson
2 Exercise C. Which of these questions will the
lecture answer? Discuss in pairs.

a Where is Oman?

b What are the major cities?

c What does the country look like?

d What is the main industry of the country?

e How many people live there?

f How can you get to the country?

2 🔲 Listen and tick the topics you hear.

3 🔲 Listen again and label the map.

C Compare your maps in pairs. Did you get the
same locations and the same spelling?

D Read the lecture on page 57. Check your answers.

E Discuss these questions in groups.

1 Have you ever visited Oman?

2 If you have, …

a where did you go?

b did you like it? Why (not)?

3 If you haven't, … would you like to go there?
Why (not)?

BAHRAIN

Arabian Gulf

QATAR

IRAN

OMAN

Gulf of Oman

Abu Dhabi

U.A.E.

OMAN

SAUDI ARABIA

Arabian Sea

YEMEN

KEY

mountains

sand desert

● capital city: _____

In this theme you are going to listen to talks about festivals.

Lesson 1: Vocabulary

You are going to learn some vocabulary you will need to understand the talks.

A Discuss these questions. Use some of the red words.

What happens in your country when someone …

1 is born?

2 has a birthday?

3 comes of age – e.g. reaches 16, 18 or 21?

4 gets married?

B Find pairs of words in the red list. Explain the connections.

Examples:

child	adult	*A child becomes an adult.*
boy	girl	*They are opposites.*

C Listen to a paragraph. Then write one of the green words in each space.

In some parts of Pakistan there are _____ events for children. The first _____ is called *Bismillah Khawni*. It takes _____ when the child is four years and four months. The boy or girl wears _____ clothes with flowers on, and family and friends watch him or her say the first chapter of the *Holy Qur'an*. The _____ ends with a special dinner. The second _____ is called *Khtme Qur'an*. This event _____ the child's ability to say the complete *Holy Qur'an*. The child receives gifts and, once again, there is a _____ dinner.

D Discuss in groups.

1 What festivals do you have in your country?

2 What does each festival celebrate?

Red words list:

adult (n)

age (n)

be born (v)

boy (n)

child (n)

congratulations (n)

dead (adj)

die (v)

family (n)

friend (n)

girl (n)

group (n)

guest (n)

live (v)

man (n)

married (adj)

name (n)

old (adj)

party (n)

people (n)

person (n)

present (n)

single (adj)

thank (v)

thank you (interj)

woman (n)

Green words list:

celebrate (v)

celebration (n)

ceremony (n)

event (n)

festival (n)

special (adj)

take place (v)

traditional (adj)

Lesson 2: Listening

A Juri Taku is a student at Greenhill College. She is going to talk to her group about a festival in Japan. Make a list of questions you expect to hear the answers to.

B 🔘 Listen to the talk once.
  1 Juri pauses a few times during her talk. Guess the word that she is going to say next. Listen and check your ideas.
  2 Tick the questions from Exercise A that she answers.

C 🔘 Listen to the talk again, without the pauses. Make notes in the table below.

Where is it?	
What is it called?	
Who is it for?	
When is it?	
Why is the occasion important?	
What happens on the day?	
Do the people wear special clothes?	
What happens after the ceremony?	

D How does Juri define these words?
  1 *Seijin-no-hi*　　**2** town hall　　**3** kimono

Revision

E Look at these words from the talk.
  <u>a</u>fter <u>a</u>ll <u>a</u>lthough c<u>a</u>lled d<u>a</u>rk f<u>i</u>rst g<u>i</u>rl h<u>a</u>ll <u>o</u>r p<u>a</u>rties p<u>e</u>rson sm<u>a</u>ll
  1 Write each word in the correct column, according to the underlined vowel sound.
  2 🔘 Listen and check your answers.

A	B	C
car	talk	word

F 🔘 What are the missing letters in each of these sentences? Listen and write the letters.
  1 I'm ___oing to talk to you about the Coming of A___e festival.
  2 It take___ ___lace on the ___econd Monday of ___anuary.
  3 It ___elebrate___ the chan___e from ___eing a child to ___eing an adult.
  4 Town hall___ are local ___overnment office___.
  5 First, official___ make speeche__.
  6 ___en they give small ___resent___.
  7 Young women wear traditional dresse___.
  8 They usually rent the kimono___.
  9 They can cost a___ much a___ a car.

Lesson 3: Learning new skills

A Think of a word to complete each sentence. Find the hidden word that connects them all.

1 We usually spend Eid days at home with the …													
2 We give children small …													
3 Sometimes on special occasions, people make …													
4 It means 'well done'.													
5 'You're 17 today! Happy … !'													
6 There are often special … in hotels at Eid.													
7 At the Coming of Age ceremony, women wear … kimonos.													
8 Do you wear special … at Eid?													

B Read these sentences from Juri's talk.
1 Write one word in each space.
  a I'm _____ to talk _____ you today _____ a festival in Japan.
  b _____, government officials make speeches.
  c _____ they give small presents to the new adults.
  d Later, _____ the ceremony, the new adults go to special parties.
  e _____, the young people go home.
2 Read Skills Check 1. Check your answers.
3 [cassette] Listen and check.

C You are going to hear two groups of words from the talk.
1 [cassette] Listen to the words in the blue box. Which consonant is missing in each case?

__alk	fes__ival
__ake	par__y
__wen__y	af__er
vo__e	la__er

2 [cassette] Listen to the words in the yellow box. Which consonant is missing in each case?

__ark	__ay
a__ult	i__ea
tra__itional	__ie
__inner	un__erstand

3 Read Skills Check 2 and check your ideas.

D Work in pairs.
1 What do all these words have in common?
   new few true blue suit you do who too
2 Read Skills Check 3. Check your answers.

Lesson 4: Applying new skills

Ⓐ Match each verb with words from the right
column to make phrases about special events.

1	give	**a**	a party
2	make	**b**	presents
3	wear	**c**	special events
4	go to	**d**	special food
5	eat	**e**	speeches
6	spend	**f**	time with the family
7	have	**g**	traditional clothes
8	listen to	**h**	special music

Ⓑ Adriana Hernandez is in Juri's group at Greenhill.
She is going to talk about a special event in
Mexico. Look at the questions in the table below.
Think of some sentences that you might hear in
Adriana's talk.

Example: a Where is the festival? *I'm going to
talk to you today about a festival in Mexico.*

9 **Ⓒ** 🔘 Listen to Adriana's talk.
1 Listen to the first part. Make notes to answer
the first seven questions.

10 **2** Listen to the second part. Complete the
information about the events in order.

a Where is the festival?		*Mexico*
b What is it called?		
c What does the name mean?		
d Who is it for?		
e When is it?		
f Why is the occasion important?		
g Do the people wear special clothes?		
h What happens on the day?	First,	
	Then,	
	After that,	
	Finally,	

Ⓓ Read the talk on page 58. Check your answers to
Exercise C.

Ⓔ When do people come of age in your country?
What happens on that day? Is there a special party?

In this theme you are going to listen to two lectures about the history of transport.

Lesson 1: Vocabulary

You are going to learn some vocabulary that you will need to understand the lectures.

A Discuss the questions. Use some of the red words.

1 Can you drive?
2 Have you passed a test?
3 Have you got a car?
4 Have you ever been in a plane? Where did you go?
5 Have you ever been on a boat? Where did you go?

B Find pairs of words in the red list. Explain the connections.

C ▭ Listen to a paragraph. Then write one of the green words or phrases in each space. Make any necessary changes.

Nowadays, we can _____ in many different ways. _____, we can _____ on a bicycle or drive in a car. In many countries, we can also go along special _____ in a train. _____, we can sail in a small boat or a large ship. _____, we can fly in a small plane or in a huge one. How did we get all these forms of _____? Who _____ them? When did each _____ happen?

D Discuss in groups. Which form of transport came first? Which is the most modern?

---

accident *(n)*
airport *(n)*
arrive *(v)*
bicycle *(n)*
boat *(n)*
bus *(n)*
bus stop *(n)*
car *(n)*
come *(v)*
drive *(v)*
driver *(n)*
fly *(v)*
go *(v)*
land *(v)*
leave *(v)*
passenger *(n)*
pilot *(n)*
plane *(n)*
road *(n)*
sail *(v)*
sailor *(n)*
ship *(n)*
street *(n)*
take off *(v)*
traffic *(n)*
train *(n)*
in the air *(prep)*
invent *(v)*
invention *(n)*
on land *(prep)*
on the sea *(prep)*
ride *(v)*
track *(n)*
transport *(n)*
travel *(v)*

Lesson 2: Listening

Ⓐ Look at these forms of transport.
  1 Number the inventions in order – the earliest = 1.
  2 Which of these inventions do you think is the greatest in the history of transport? Discuss in groups.

Ⓑ Vicente Fernandez is studying History at Greenhill College. He has a lecture today.
  1 🔊 What is the lecturer going to talk about? Look at the notebook. Listen and number the points in order.
  2 Which word or phrase does he define as:
    a new way of doing something?
    b area?
    c types?
    d in my opinion?
    🔊 Listen again and check your answers.
  3 🔊 Listen to the second part. When the lecturer stops, guess the next word. Then check your guesses.
  4 🔊 Copy Table 1. Then listen to the third part and complete the table.
  5 🔊 Listen to the final part.
    a Which invention does the lecturer think is the most important invention?
    b Why does he have this opinion?

Ⓒ 🔊 Listen to the third part of the lecture again. Copy and complete Table 1 with dates and names.

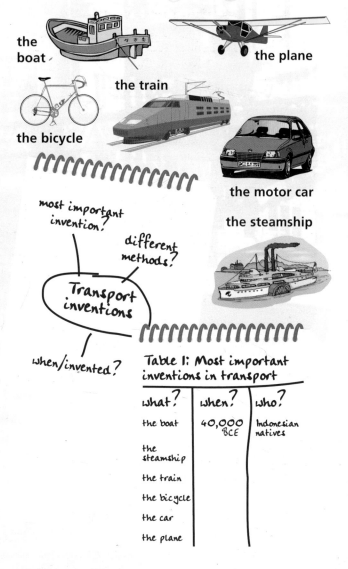

the boat · the plane · the train · the bicycle · the motor car · the steamship

most important invention?

different methods?

Transport inventions

when/invented?

Table I: Most important inventions in transport

what?	when?	who?
the boat	40,000 BCE	Indonesian natives
the steamship		
the train		
the bicycle		
the car		
the plane		

Revision

Ⓓ Look at these words from the talk. They all have short vowel sounds.
  1 Write each word in the correct column, according to the (underlined) vowel.
  2 🔊 Listen and check your answers.

because engine engine history that track transport was went what when which wind

A	B	C	D
ship	land	tell	on

Ⓔ Look at these words from the talk. They all have long vowel sounds in British English.
  1 Write each word in the correct column, according to the (underlined) vowel.
  2 🔊 Listen and check your answers.

after called concerned course each far flew last more move people steam transport use walk world

A	B	C	D	E
sea	car	first	talk	new

Lesson 3: Learning new skills

A Think of a word to complete each sentence. Find the hidden word that connects them all.

1 and **2** – Karl Benz invented it. (2 words)	**1**												
	2												
3 You can do this on two legs.	**3**												
4 The Wright Brothers flew the first one successfully.	**4**												
5 and **6** – J.C. Perier invented it in 1775 to sail on the sea. (2 words)	**5**												
	6												
7 It is more than 40,000 years old.	**7**												
8 All the other answers are different ways of …	**8**												
9 The Rocket was the engine that pulled the first …	**9**												

B Read the introduction to the lecture in Lesson 2.

1 Write one word in each space.

> I'm _____ to _____ to you today about inventions. _____, I'm going to talk _____ different methods of transport. After _____, I'll _____ you when each method was invented. _____, I'm going to _____ which invention was the most important. _____ , first, what are the main methods of transport?

2 🎧 Listen to the introduction again and check your answers.

3 Read Skills Check 1. Notice the signposts in the introduction.

C Vicente started to make notes during the introduction. Has he organized them well? Explain your answer.

Inventions in transport

Different methods   *When?*

Most important?

D What are the missing letters – *sh* or *ch*?

1 Work out the missing letters.

2 🎧 Listen and check your ideas.

a ___eck   **e** mu___
b ea___   **f** ___ip
c Engli___   **g** ___ort
d mat___   **h** whi___

E You have heard all the words below in the course.

1 What do the words have in common? Which is the odd one out?

invention	conversation	congratulations
action	definition	information
celebration	description	connection
civilization	question	location
condition	education	

2 Read Skills Check 3. Check your answers.

Lesson 4: Applying new skills

Ⓐ Work in pairs. Look at these flying machines. Match the names to the machines.

__ helicopter
__ jet
__ jumbo jet
__ plane
__ space rocket
__ space shuttle

Ⓑ Vicente has another lecture on his history course.
1 Look at the way he has organised his notes. What order does he think the information will be in?
2 🔊 Listen to the introduction. Correct Vicente's work.

Ⓒ 🔊 Listen to the second part of the lecture. When the lecturer stops, guess the next word. Then check your guesses.

Ⓓ 🔊 Listen to the third part of the lecture. How does the lecturer define these words?
1 propeller
2 jet
3 jumbo
4 shuttle

Ⓔ 🔊 Listen to the third part again. Complete Table 1 with inventions, dates and names.

Ⓕ 🔊 Listen to the final part.
1 Which invention does the lecturer think is the most important?
2 Why does she have this opinion?

Ⓖ Discuss these questions in groups.
1 Which do you think was the most important invention in flying? Why?
2 Which types of flying machine have you been in? When?
3 Which would you like / hate to go in? Why?

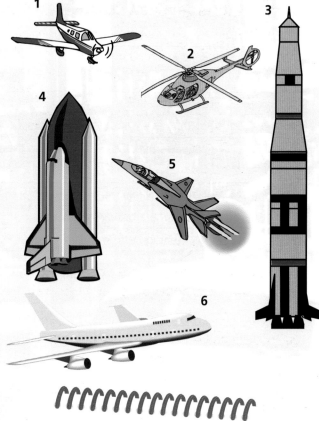

Inventions in flying

What?   When?   Who?

Most important?

Table 1: Most important inventions in flying

What?	When?	Who?
the plane		Wright brothers
the jet engine	1930	Frank _____
the jumbo jet	1970	
the helicopter		Igor Sikorsky
the space rocket		Robert Goddard
the space shuttle	1976	

In this theme you are going to hear two radio programmes about traditional stories. You are also going to hear two stories.

Lesson 1: Vocabulary

You are going to learn some vocabulary that you will need to understand the radio programmes and the stories.

Ⓐ Discuss these questions.

1 Do you like reading? What sort of books do you like best?

2 Do you like films? Do you tell your friends the story of a film you have seen?

Ⓑ Look at the red words. They are all infinitives of verbs.

1 Find and underline all the regular verbs.

2 How do you pronounce the past tense in each case? Write the verb in the correct column of Table 1.

3 📼 Listen and check your ideas.

Table 1: Regular past tense sounds

A	B	C
checked	carried	ended
/t/	/d/	/ɪd/

Ⓒ Look at the rest of the red words. They are infinitives of irregular verbs.

1 What is the past tense of each verb? Discuss in pairs.

2 📼 Listen to 15 irregular past tense verbs. Write the number of the past tense verb you hear next to the correct infinitive in the list of red words.

Ⓓ 📼 Listen to a paragraph. Then write one of the green words in each space. Everybody likes a good _____. There are _____ in the _____ of every culture. Children learn them at home or at school. Many of these stories have a _____ – in other words, a lesson for life. For example, help people and they will help you. There is usually one main _____ – one person who does most of the actions. We often don't know the name of the _____ of these traditional stories. People often _____ the best stories into many languages so, in the end, the same story _____ all around the world.

bring *(v)*
build *(v)*
carry *(v)*
check *(v)*
climb *(v)*
come *(v)*
do *(v)*
draw *(v)*
end *(v)*
feel *(v)*
find *(v)*
get *(v)*
give *(v)*
go *(v)*
leave *(v)*
live *(v)*
look *(v)*
make *(v)*
meet *(v)*
move *(v)*
point *(v)*
put *(v)*
run *(v)*
say *(v)*
send *(v)*
start *(v)*
stop *(v)*
take *(v)*
talk *(v)*
tell *(v)*
walk *(v)*
want *(v)*
appear *(v)*
character *(n)*
literature *(n)*
moral *(n)*
stories *(n)*
story *(n)*
translate *(v)*
writer *(n)*

Lesson 2: Listening

Ⓐ Look at the pictures in Lesson 1. Have you heard of these characters? What stories do you know about them? What is the connection between all three characters?

Ⓑ You are going to hear part of a radio programme. Read the information and answer the questions.
1 What is this programme about?
2 Who is the presenter?
3 What are you going to hear on the programme?

Ⓒ Here are some statements about *The Arabian Nights*.
1 Decide if each sentence is true or false.
  a *The Arabian Nights* is also called *The Hundred and One Nights*.
  b Stories are from different countries.
  c An Egyptian wrote down all the stories.
  d Aladdin found a lamp.
  e Sindbad had problems with 40 thieves.
  f *The Arabian Nights* is well-known in the Western World.
2 🔊 Listen to the first part of the programme and check your answers.

Ⓓ 🔊 Listen again. Complete the table.
Table 1: History of The Arabian Nights

Date	Event	Writer
	some stories appeared	anonymous
1500	stories written down	an Egyptian
	translated: Arabic ➜	
1885	translated: Arabic ➜	

Ⓔ How does Jenny define these words / phrases?
anonymous folklore generation to generation

Ⓕ 🔊 Listen to the story. Which sentence about the story is true?
1 At the end of the story, the poor man knew a thief took his donkey.
2 The thief changed into a donkey because he hit his mother.
3 The poor man was a nice man but a little stupid.
4 At the end of the story, the poor man got his donkey back.

9.30 Literature around the world

This week, Jenny Ingram talks about the history of *The Arabian Nights*. She also introduces one of the stories from the collection, *The Thieves and the Donkey.*

Revision

Ⓖ Here are words from the radio programme.
1 🔊 Listen to the words in Column A.
2 🔊 Listen to the words in the orange box. Write each word in a space in Column B.
3 🔊 Write each word from the yellow box in a space in Column C. Listen and check.

A	B	C
lived		
means		
led		
words		
man		
passed		
not		
called		
young		
rude		
took		

back bought his looked market mother problem thief went who world

bird English father few lamp put said son steal stopped story

Lesson 3: Learning new skills

(A) Discuss. In the story in Lesson 2 ...

1 how many characters are there?

2 who are the characters?

3 which collection does it come from?

4 who wrote the collection?

(B) Can you remember the story?

1 Tell the story in pairs.

2 Make a note of every past simple verb from the story.

3 Choose 5 of these past simple verbs. Make a new sentence with each.

(C) In the story from Lesson 2, there is ...

1 a young man / thief.

2 an old man / thief.

3 a poor man.

🔊 Who did what? Listen to the story in Lesson 2 again. Answer each question with 1, 2 or 3.

a __ Who saw a poor man at the market?

b __ Who went up behind the poor man?

c __ Who untied the rope from the donkey and put it around his own neck?

d __ Who took the donkey away?

e __ Who suddenly stopped?

f __ Who said, 'Who are you'?

g __ Who said, 'I am your donkey'?

h __ Who untied the rope?

i __ Who said, 'Go back to your home?'

j __ Who was surprised to see the donkey for sale again?

k __ Who said, 'I told you not to be rude to your mother again'?

(D) 🔊 Look at these words from the talk. Listen. Tick the correct column, according to the stressed vowel sound.

	1	2
	night	day
away		
became		
behind		
buy		
eighty		
famous		
generation		
made		
tie		
time		
translate		

Skills Check 1

Following a narrative (1)

You must understand *who* did *what*.

1 If there are two or three men or women in a story, narrators use adjectives **in front of** the noun. Listen for:

age *a young man, an old man*

appearance *a big man, a small man*

other description *a rich man, a poor man*, etc.

2 Sometimes narrators give you extra information **after** the noun.

appearance *a man with a beard*

possessions *a man with a donkey*

3 Sometimes narrators tell you the **occupation** of a character.

occupation *a policeman, a thief*, etc.

4 Sometimes narrators use different words for the same character:

Example:

Once there were two **thieves**, ...

a young man and **an old man**.

5 Listen also for the pronouns. You must understand who each pronoun refers to.

Example:

Once there were two **thieves**, ...

They *were at a market.*

Skills Check 2

Hearing diphthongs with /ɪ/

There are three diphthongs (or double vowels) ending in /ɪ/.

/aɪ/ – *night, why, find*

/eɪ/ – *day, wait, make*

/ɔɪ/ – *boy, toy, oil*

Lesson 4: Applying new skills

A You are going to hear part of a radio programme. Read the information and answer the questions.
1 What is this programme about?
2 What is a *wise fool*?
3 What are you going to hear on the programme?

B 🎧 Listen to the first part of the programme. Complete the table.

Table 1: 'Wise Fool' stories around the world

Country	Name of character	Dates
Greece		/
China		/
Turkey	Hodja /	1208 –
Arab World	or	c.

C Do you know the story of *Joha and the Donkey*?
1 What can you remember about it?
2 🎧 Listen and compare your ideas with this version.

D Work in pairs. Read the sentences below.
1 Who said each sentence?
2 Who does each pronoun refer to?

a He has no respect for his father.

b Father, you must ride on the donkey and I will walk.

c He has no feeling for his son.

d Son, we must both ride.

e They have no feeling for their donkey.

f We must carry the donkey.

g Why aren't they riding it?

E Some stories have a moral. What is the moral of this story?

9.30 Literature around the world

This week, Jenny Ingram talks about stories of a wise fool – in other words, a person who does silly things but has a clever reason for them. Where did the stories start? Was there ever a real wise fool? She also introduces one of the stories, *Joha and the Donkey*.

THEME 9 Sports and Leisure — Classifying Sports

In this theme you are going to listen to two lectures about sports.

Lesson 1: Vocabulary

You are going to learn some vocabulary you will need to understand the lectures.

A Discuss these questions. Use some of the red words.

    1 What do you do in your spare time?

    2 What sort of things do you read regularly?

    3 What sports do you play?

    4 What sports do you watch?

B Complete the crossword. Use red and green words.
Find the hidden place that links all the answers.

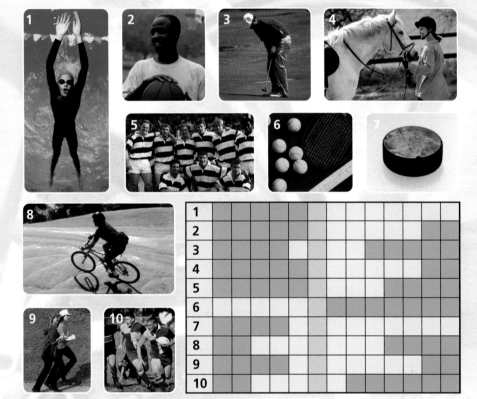

C 🔊 Listen to a paragraph. Then write one of the red or green words in each space. Change the form of the word if necessary.

There are many different kinds of _____. We play some sports with a _____ – for example, football, tennis, _____ and _____. We _____ some sports with other _____ in a team. For example, football is a _____ sport. Sometimes we need a piece of _____ to take part in a sport. We need a bicycle, of course, for _____, and we need a stick for _____.

D Discuss in groups.
Where can you do these things in your town or city?

    1 play football   **4** play ice hockey

    2 play tennis   **5** go riding

    3 play golf   **6** go cycling

---

ball (n)

baseball (n)

beach (n)

film (n and v)

football (n)

hobby (n)

magazine (n)

news (n)

newspaper (n)

play (n and v)

programme (n)

radio (n)

show (n)

sport (n)

sports (n)

swimming (n)

tennis (n)

theatre (n)

turn off (v)

turn on (v)

watch (v)

cycling (n)

equipment (n)

golf (n)

ice hockey (n)

player (n)

riding (n)

rugby (n)

running (n)

team (n)

Lesson 2: Listening

A Put these sports into groups. Explain your choices.

cycling	motor racing
football	running
golf	swimming
long jump	tennis

long jump   **motor racing**   **golf**

B Manuel Molinero is studying Sports Education at Greenhill College.
He has a lecture today about different types of sports.

1 🔲 Listen to the introduction. Write the missing words in *Categories* and *Definitions*.

2 🔲 Listen to Part 2. When the lecturer stops, guess the next word. Then listen and check.

3 🔲 Listen to Part 2 again. Complete the *Sub-categories* section with headings under each arrow.

4 🔲 Listen to Part 2 again and write one example for each sub-category.

5 🔲 Listen to the summary of the lecture (Part 3) and check your answers.

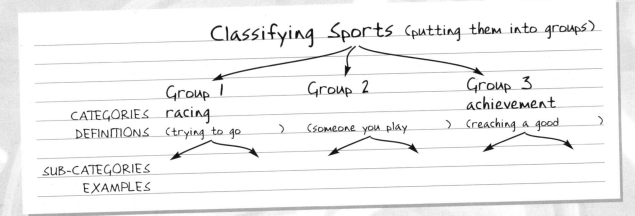

C Write as examples of other sports of each sub-category.

Revision

D All these words from the lecture contain the vowel letter *a*. But what is the sound in each word?

1 Tick under the word with the same vowel sound.

2 🔲 Listen and check your answers.

	1	2	3	4	5	6	7	8
	/iː/	/æ/	/ɑː/	/ɒ/	/ɔː/	/e/	/ɜː/	/eɪ/
ag<u>ai</u>nst								
b<u>a</u>ll								
cl<u>a</u>ss								
he<u>a</u>rd								
qu<u>a</u>ntity								
r<u>a</u>cing								
re<u>a</u>ch								
t<u>a</u>rget								
te<u>a</u>m								
th<u>a</u>t								

Lesson 3: Learning new skills

A How can a lecturer tell listeners that a word is important?
1 Think of at least three ways.
2 Read Skills Check 1. Check your ideas.

> He can say, "This word is important!"

> She can say the word more slowly.

B 🔊 Listen to Part 1 of the lecture from Lesson 2 again. Put your hand up when you hear an important word.

C 🔊 Listen to Part 2 of the lecture again. How does the lecturer show that these words are important? Tick one or more ways.

key word	slowly	loudly	explanation	example	repetition
racing	✓	✓	✓	✓	✓
machine					
opponent					
person					
target					
quantity					

D Look at these words from the lecture.
1 Do they have the sound in *no* or the sound in *now*? Tick in one column for each word.
2 🔊 Listen and check your ideas.

	A	B
	no	now
	/əʊ/	/aʊ/
so		
p<u>o</u>wer		
opp<u>o</u>nent		
how		
know		
go		
also		
OK		

Recognising important words

It is impossible to hear and understand everything that a lecturer says in a foreign language. You must decide which words are important and then check the meaning later, if necessary. The lecturer usually helps you to recognise important words. He / she does one or more of these things:
1 says the word **more slowly**.
2 says the word **more loudly**.
3 **explains** the meaning of the words.
4 gives an **example** of the word in use.
   Don't worry if you do not hear the word clearly the first time. A good lecturer usually …
5 **repeats** important words.

Skills Check 2

Hearing vowels – *no* and *now*

These two diphthongs are very similar.
Examples:
hole, go, so, OK
how, now, power

Lesson 4: Applying new skills

A Look at these balls. Which sport do you play with each one? Join each word to the correct ball.

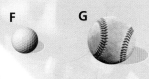

1 baseball
2 basketball
3 football
4 golf
5 rugby
6 tennis
7 volleyball
8 cricket

B Manuel has another lecture on his Sports Education course.
1 Look at his notes. How does he think the lecture will be organised?
2 🔊 Listen to the introduction. Listen for the important words. Correct Manuel's work below.

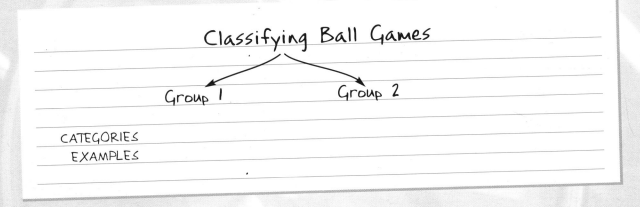

Classifying Ball Games

Group 1   Group 2

CATEGORIES
EXAMPLES

C 🔊 Listen to Part 2. When the lecturer stops, guess the next word. Then listen and check.

D 🔊 Listen to Part 2 again.
1 Write the missing words in *Categories*.
2 Write the ball games from Exercise 1 in the correct categories. For Group 3, write the name of the bat in brackets after each game.
3 Add one more game to Group 1 and Group 3.

E 🔊 Listen to Part 3. Discuss in pairs.
1 Why is it important to classify ball games in this way?
2 What must Manuel do before the next lecture?

F Which of the sports in this lesson …
1 do you understand?
2 can you play?
3 do you like watching?

In this theme you are going to listen to two lectures about food groups and healthy eating.

Lesson 1: Vocabulary

You are going to learn some vocabulary you will need to understand the lectures.

A Do the quiz. It uses some of the red words.

The FOOD *quiz*

Name as many foods as you can.
You have one minute for each one.

1 drinks_____

_____

2 fruit_____

_____

3 vegetables _____

_____

4 meat _____

_____

B  Listen to a paragraph. Then write one of the red or green words in each space.

Why do we eat? What a silly question! We eat because we are _____. Well, that answer is true, in a way. But why do we feel hungry? We feel hungry because the _____ needs more energy. The whole body needs _____ to move. Every part of the body needs energy to work correctly. We get energy from _____. However, we have to be careful. If we don't use all the energy from food, the _____ keeps it. How does it keep it? It keeps it as _____. It is easy to use *new* energy from _____. It is much harder to use the _____ in fat. So, what's the answer? We must eat the right *amount* of _____, and we must take _____ to use the extra energy. The food we normally eat is called our _____. Of course, we must eat the right *kind* of food as well. If we eat the right amount of the right kind of food, we will have a healthy _____. But what's the right *kind* of food? That's another question.

C The paragraph talks about the problems of too *much* food. Can you have too *little* food? What happens (if anything)?

bottle *(n)*
bread *(n)*
breakfast *(n)*
butter *(n)*
cheese *(n)*
chicken *(n)*
coffee *(n)*
cup *(n)*
dentist *(n)*
drink *(n and v)*
eat *(n)*
egg *(n)*
food *(n)*
fruit *(n)*
glass *(n)*
ice-cream *(n)*
jam *(n)*
juice *(n)*
meal *(n)*
meat *(n)*
menu *(n)*
milk *(n)*
restaurant *(n)*
rice *(n)*
salad *(n)*
salt *(n)*
sandwich *(n)*
sugar *(n)*
tea *(n)*
vegetable *(n)*
body *(n)*
diet *(n)*
energy *(n)*
exercise *(n)*
fat *(n)*
hungry *(adj)*

Lesson 2: Listening review (1)

A Look at the names of foods in the box.

apples beef butter bread carrots cheese chicken eggs lamb milk oranges pasta peas rice

1 Put the foods into groups. Explain your choices.

2 Add some more foods to each group.

B 🔊 Noura Hamed is studying Food Sciences at Greenhill College. She has a lecture today about food. Listen to the first part. When the lecturer stops, guess the next word. Did you guess correctly?

C Read this summary of the first part.

1 Complete the notes.

2 🔊 Listen to the first part again and check.

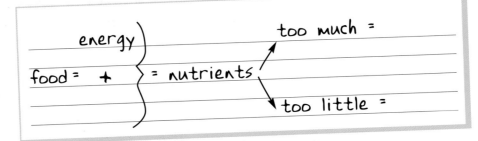

D 🔊 Listen to the second part. What is the lecturer going to talk about this week? Tick one or more.

☐ food groups
☐ foods that contain each nutrient
☐ how much food you need from each group
☐ different nutrients

E Look at Table 1.

1 Look at the name of the first nutrient. Do you know the names of the other four?

2 🔊 Listen to the third part and complete the names of the nutrients.

3 Look at the foods. Do you know, or can you guess, which foods contain each nutrient? Many foods contain more than one. Tick any boxes that apply.

4 🔊 Listen to the fourth part. Check and complete the table.

Table 1: Nutrients in particular foods

		NUTRIENTS				
		carbohydrates				
FOOD	bread	✓				
	cheese					
	eggs					
	fish					
	fruit					
	meat					
	milk					
	pasta					
	rice					
	vegetables					

F 🔊 Listen to the fifth part. What does the lecturer want you to do before next week?

G How often do you eat each of the foods in Table 1? All the time? Occasionally? Never?

Lesson 3: Listening review (2)

A You can complete each phrase on the right from the lecture with a preposition or adverb.

1 Write a preposition or adverb in each space.

2 🔾🔾 Listen and check your ideas.

a	talk	*about*
b	take energy	
c	the parts	
d	different types	
e	too much	
f	some examples	
g	find carbohydrates	
h	look	(on the Internet)
i	look	
j	make some notes	
k	do research	
l	note some things	

B Can you remember any sentences from the lecture that contain the phrases in Exercise A?

Example: *There are several **different types of** nutrients.*

C In this course you have learnt to hear different sounds.

1 All these words are in the lecture. Find the odd one out from each group in standard British English. (Think about the [underlined] vowel sound.)

2 🔾🔾 Listen and check your ideas.

a	t<u>a</u>lk	w<u>o</u>rk	c<u>ou</u>rse	c<u>a</u>ll
b	t<u>y</u>pe	r<u>i</u>ce	g<u>i</u>ve	f<u>i</u>nally
c	m<u>ai</u>n	cont<u>ai</u>n	h<u>a</u>ve	t<u>a</u>ke
d	s<u>o</u>	kn<u>o</u>w	d<u>oe</u>s	n<u>o</u>te
e	m<u>ea</u>t	ch<u>ee</u>se	br<u>ea</u>d	prot<u>ei</u>n
f	n<u>u</u>trient	fr<u>ui</u>t	m<u>u</u>ch	f<u>oo</u>d
g	<u>a</u>bout	am<u>ou</u>nt	h<u>o</u>w	gr<u>ou</u>p

D In this course you have learnt to understand spoken spellings.

1 🔾🔾 Listen to the spelling of more words from the lecture. Write the letters.

2 Can you identify each word?

E In this course you have learnt to understand spoken definitions.

1 🔾🔾 Listen again to part of the lecture. Which words does the lecturer define?

2 🔾🔾 Listen again. Make notes of the definition of each word.

F In this course you have learnt to recognise important words.

1 Read this part of the lecture. Underline the words you think are important.

2 🔾🔾 Listen and check your ideas.

We call the energy and chemicals in food 'nutrients'. As you probably know, there are several different types of nutrient. The body needs different amounts of each nutrient. If you have too much of a particular type, you can get fat. If you have too little of a particular type, you can get ill.

Lesson 4: Listening review (3)

Ⓐ What is a healthy diet? Number these types of food in order.
1 = you should eat very little of this, 6 = you should eat a lot of this.
___ fats
___ meat and fish
___ vegetables
___ fruit
___ eggs, milk, cheese
___ carbohydrates

Ⓑ 🔘 Noura has another lecture on her Food Sciences course. Listen to the first part. When the lecturer stops, guess the next word. Did you guess correctly?

Ⓒ What is the lecturer going to talk about this week?
1 Complete the notes.
2 🔘 Listen to the first part again and check.

1. food _____ = a group of _____ = 6; some are the same as _____, some are diff.

2. healthy eating = groups together in _____ way

3. own _____

Ⓓ The lecturer is going to explain the six food groups.
1 Can you guess what the six food groups are?
2 🔘 Listen to the second part and check your ideas.
3 One group has a special name. What is it?

Ⓔ Look at Figure 1 below.
1 What is the lecturer going to talk about next?
2 🔘 Listen to the third part and check your ideas.
3 🔘 Listen to the third part again and complete the figure. Copy the spelling of the words from Exercise A. Shade or colour in the squares.
4 Look back at your answer to Exercise A. Did you get it right?

Ⓕ 🔘 Listen to the last part of the lecture. What does the lecturer want you to do?

Ⓖ Follow the lecturer's instructions.
Figure 1: The balanced diet pyaramid

Fats										
Dairy products										
										Fruit

Word Lists: Thematic

THEME 1
Education, Student Life

answer (n and v)

ask (v)

begin (v)

dictionary (n)

end (v)

explain (v)

history (n)

learn (v)

listen (v)

mathematics (n)

question (n)

read (v)

right (adj)

science (n)

spell (v)

student (n)

study (v)

teach (v)

test (n and v)

university (n)

write (v)

wrong (adj)

academic (adj)

college (n)

head (n)

in charge (of) (adj)

lecture (n)

principal (n)

responsible (for) (adj)

semester (n)

subject (n)

term (n)

THEME 2
Daily Life, Schedules

afternoon (n)

autumn (n)

day (n)

evening (n)

first (adj)

hour (n)

last (adj)

late (adj)

later (adj)

midnight (n)

minute (n)

month (n)

morning (n)

night (n)

noon (n)

now (adv)

o'clock (adv)

past (adv and n)

quarter (n)

spring (n)

summer (n)

time (n)

today (n)

tomorrow (n)

tonight (n)

week (n)

winter (n)

year (n)

yesterday (n)

campus (n)

chess (n)

club (n)

film (n)

music (n)

plan (v)

restaurant (n)

sports (n)

THEME 3
Work and Business, Work Starts Now!

company (n)

computer (n)

desk (n)

e-mail (n)

envelope (n)

factory (n)

file (n)

job (n)

letter (n)

manager (n)

office (n)

secretary (n)

shelf / shelves (n)

shop (n)

start (v)

supermarket (n)

typist (n)

website (n)

work (n and v)

working hours (n)

colleague (n)

papers (n)

product (n)

rely on (v)

salary (n)

service (n)

urgent (adj)

THEME 4
Science and Nature, So You Want to Be a Scientist?

black (adj)

blue (adj)

brown (adj)

cold (adj)

colour (n and v)

cloud (n)

flower (n)

fog (n)

forest (n)

grass (n)

green (adj)

grey (adj)

hot (adj)

island (n)

lake (n)

mountain (n)

orange (adj)

rain (n and v)

red (adj)

river (n)

sea (n)

sky (n)

snow (n and v)

sun (n)

temperature (n)

thunderstorm (n)

tree (n)

water (n)

weather (n)

white (adj)

wind (n)

yellow (adj)

graph (n)

laboratory (n)

science (n)

scientific (adj)

scientist (n)

table (n)

test (v)

THEME 5
The Physical World, Where Is Your Country?

behind (prep)

between (prep)

corner (n)

country (n)

east (n)

in front of (prep)

in the centre of (prep)

left (n)

mountain (n)

near (prep)

next to (prep)

north (n)

opposite (prep)

south (n)

town (n)

west (n)

border (n and v)

continent (n)

locate (v)

location (n)

the Equator (n)

the Tropic of Cancer (n)

the Tropic of Capricorn (n)

THEME 6
Culture and Civilization, Congratulations!

adult (n)

age (n)

be born (v)

boy (n)

child (n)

congratulations (n)

dead (adj)

die (v)

family (n)

friend (n)

girl (n)

group (n)

guest (n)

live (v)

man (n)

married (adj)

name (n)

old (adj)

party (n)

people (n)

person (n)

present (n)

single (adj)

thank (v)

thank you (interj)

woman (n)

celebrate (v)

celebration (n)

ceremony (n)

event (n)

festival (n)

special (adj)

take place (v)

traditional (adj)

THEME 7
They Made Our World, Who? What? When?

accident (n)

airport (n)

arrive (v)

bicycle (n)

boat (n)

bus (n)

bus stop (n)

car (n)

come (v)

drive (v)

driver (n)

fly (v)

go (v)

land (v)

leave (v)

passenger (n)

pilot (n)

plane (n)

road (n)

sail (v)

sailor (n)

ship (n)

street (n)

take off (v)

traffic (n)

train (n)

in the air (prep)

invent (v)

invention (n)

on land (prep)

on the sea (prep)

ride (v)

track (n)

transport (n)

travel (v)

THEME 8
Art and Literature, There Was Once a Poor Man …

bring (v)

build (v)

carry (v)

check (v)

climb (v)

come (v)

do (v)

draw (v)

end (v)

feel (v)

find (v)

get (v)

give (v)

go (v)

leave (v)

live (v)

look (v)

make (v)

meet (v)

move (v)

point (v)

put (v)

run (v)

say (v)

send (v)

start (v)

stop (v)

take (v)

talk (v)

tell (v)

walk (v)

want (v)

appear (v)

character (n)

literature (n)

moral (n)

stories (n)

story (n)

translate (v)

writer (n)

THEME 9
Sports and Leisure, Classifying Sports

ball *(n)*

baseball *(n)*

beach *(n)*

film *(n and v)*

football *(n)*

hobby *(n)*

magazine *(n)*

news *(n)*

newspaper *(n)*

play *(n and v)*

programme *(n)*

radio *(n)*

show *(n)*

sport *(n)*

sports *(n)*

swimming *(n)*

tennis *(n)*

theatre *(n)*

turn off *(v)*

turn on *(v)*

watch *(v)*

cycling *(n)*

equipment *(n)*

golf *(n)*

ice hockey *(n)*

player *(n)*

riding *(n)*

rugby *(n)*

running *(n)*

team *(n)*

THEME 10
Nutrition and Health, Nutrients and Food Groups

bottle *(n)*

bread *(n)*

breakfast *(n)*

butter *(n)*

cheese *(n)*

chicken *(n)*

coffee *(n)*

cup *(n)*

dentist *(n)*

drink *(n and v)*

eat *(n)*

egg *(n)*

food *(n)*

fruit *(n)*

glass *(n)*

ice-cream *(n)*

jam *(n)*

juice *(n)*

meal *(n)*

meat *(n)*

menu *(n)*

milk *(n)*

restaurant *(n)*

rice *(n)*

salad *(n)*

salt *(n)*

sandwich *(n)*

sugar *(n)*

tea *(n)*

vegetable *(n)*

body *(n)*

diet *(n)*

energy *(n)*

exercise *(n)*

fat *(n)*

hungry *(adj)*

academic *(adj)*

accident *(n)*

adult *(n)*

afternoon *(n)*

age *(n)*

airport *(n)*

answer *(n and v)*

appear *(v)*

arrive *(v)*

ask *(v)*

autumn *(n)*

ball *(n)*

baseball *(n)*

be born *(v)*

beach *(n)*

begin *(v)*

behind *(prep)*

between *(prep)*

bicycle *(n)*

black *(adj)*

blue *(adj)*

boat *(n)*

body *(n)*

border *(n and v)*

bottle *(n)*

boy *(n)*

bread *(n)*

breakfast *(n)*

bring *(v)*

brown *(adj)*

build *(v)*

bus *(n)*

bus stop *(n)*

butter *(n)*

campus *(n)*

car *(n)*

carry *(v)*

celebrate *(v)*

celebration *(n)*

ceremony *(n)*

character *(n)*

check *(v)*

cheese *(n)*

chess *(n)*

chicken *(n)*

child *(n)*

climb *(v)*

cloud *(n)*

club *(n)*

coffee *(n)*

cold *(adj)*

colleague *(n)*

college *(n)*

colour *(n and v)*

come *(v)*

company *(n)*

computer *(n)*

congratulations *(n)*

continent *(v)*

corner *(n)*

country *(n)*

cup *(n)*

cycling *(n)*

day *(n)*

dead *(adj)*

dentist *(n)*

desk *(n)*

dictionary *(n)*

die *(v)*

diet *(n)*

do *(v)*

draw *(v)*

drink *(n and v)*

drive *(v)*

driver *(n)*

east *(n)*

eat *(v)*

egg *(n)*

e-mail *(n)*

end *(v)*

energy *(n)*

envelope *(n)*

equipment (n)
evening (n)
event (n)
exercise (n)
explain (v)
factory (n)
family (n)
fat (n)
feel (v)
festival (n)
file (n)
film (n and v)
film (n)
find (v)
first (adj)
flower (n)
fly (v)
fog (n)
food (n)
football (n)
forest (n)
friend (n)
fruit (n)
get (v)
girl (n)
give (v)
glass (n)
go (v)
golf (n)
graph (n)
grass (n)
green (adj)
grey (adj)
group (n)
guest (n)
head (n)
history (n)
hobby (n)
hot (adj)
hour (n)
hungry (adj)

ice hockey (n)
ice-cream (n)
in charge (of) (adj)
in front of (prep)
in the air (prep)
in the centre of (prep)
invent (v)
invention (n)
island (n)
jam (n)
job (n)
juice (n)
laboratory (n)
lake (n)
land (v)
last (adj)
late (adj)
later (adj)
learn (v)
leave (v)
lecture (n)
left (n)
letter (n)
listen (v)
literature (n)
live (v)
locate (v)
location (n)
look (v)
magazine (n)
make (v)
man (n)
manager (n)
married (adj)
mathematics (n)
meal (n)
meat (n)
meet (v)
menu (n)
midnight (n)
milk (n)

minute (n)
month (n)
moral (n)
morning (n)
mountain (n)
move (v)
music (n)
name (n)
near (prep)
news (n)
newspaper (n)
next to (prep)
night (n)
noon (n)
north (n)
now (adj)
o'clock (adv)
office (n)
old (adj)
on land (prep)
on the sea (prep)
opposite (prep)
orange (adj)
papers (n)
party (n)
passenger (n)
past (adv and n)
people (n)
person (n)
pilot (n)
plan (n)
plane (n)
play (n and v)
player (n)
point (v)
present (n)
principal (n)
product (n)
programme (n)
put (v)
quarter (n)

question (n)
radio (n)
rain (n and v)
read (v)
red (adj)
rely on (v)
responsible (for) (adj)
restaurant (n)
restaurant (n)
rice (n)
ride (v)
riding (n)
right (adj)
river (n)
road (n)
rugby (n)
run (v)
running (n)
sail (v)
sailor (n)
salad (n)
salary (n)
salt (n)
sandwich (n)
say (v)
science (n)
science (n)
scientific (adj)
scientist (n)
sea (n)
secretary (n)
semester (n)
send (v)
service (n)
shelf / shelves (n)
ship (n)
shop (n)
show (n)
single (adj)
sky (n)
snow (n and v)

south (n)

special (adj)

spell (v)

sport (n)

sports (n)

sports (n)

spring (n)

start (v)

stop (v)

stories (n)

story (n)

street (n)

student (n)

study (v)

subject (n)

sugar (n)

summer (n)

sun (n)

supermarket (n)

swimming (n)

table (n)

take off (v)

take place (v)

talk (v)

tea (n)

teach (v)

team (n)

tell (v)

temperature (n)

tennis (n)

term (n)

test (n and v)

test (v)

thank (v)

thank you (interj)

theatre (n)

the Equator (n)

the Tropic of Cancer (n)

the Tropic of Capricorn (n)

thunderstorm (n)

time (n)

today (n)

tomorrow (n)

tonight (n)

town (n)

track (n)

traditional (adj)

traffic (n)

train (n)

translate (v)

transport (n)

travel (v)

tree (n)

turn off (v)

turn on (v)

typist (n)

university (n)

urgent (adj)

vegetable (n)

walk (v)

want (v)

watch (v)

water (n)

weather (n)

website (n)

week (n)

west (n)

white (adj)

wind (n)

winter (n)

woman (n)

work (n and v)

working hours (n)

write (v)

writer (n)

wrong (adj)

year (n)

yellow (adj)

yesterday (n)

Presenter: Theme 1: Education, Student Life
Lesson 1: **Vocabulary**
B Listen to some sentences with the green words. Then complete each sentence with one of the words.

Voice: 1 The academic year in my country starts in October. All the students go back to high school then.
2 When does the second semester start? Is it in February?
3 Which room is the lecture in? The one about· learning English?
4 Mr Jones is in charge of the library. He is responsible for all the books and CD-ROMs.
5 Who is the head of Year 1? Is it Mrs Wright? Or is she in charge of Year 2?

Presenter: Lesson 2: **Listening**
C It is the start of the college year at Greenhill College. The principal is welcoming the new students. Listen and add the missing information.

Peter Bean: OK. Let's begin. Welcome to Greenhill College. I am very pleased to see you all here. My name is Peter Bean. I'm the principal – that means I am in charge of the whole place. You come and see me if you have any problems with the fees – that means the money you must pay. My office is on the first floor, Room 15, by the stairs. The people behind me are some of my staff. This is Mrs Polly Penn. She's the head of Year 1. She is responsible for the schedule. After this meeting, Mrs Penn will give you the schedule for the first term. The schedule tells you the times of all your lectures. Mrs Penn will also give you the name of your instructor. We call the teachers at Greenhill instructors. She will also tell you the name of your personal advisor*** – that's a person who helps you if you have problems. Finally, this is the registrar, Mr Bill Beale. He's in charge of attendance. If you can't come to college one day, tell Mr Beale. OK, that's it from me. Now I'll hand over to Mrs Penn … Oh, I nearly forgot. Mr Beale's room is on the first floor, next to my room – Room 16.

Presenter: **E The principal explains the meaning of each word in Exercise D. Listen to his speech again and check your answers.**
[REPEAT OF LESSON 2 EXERCISE C]

Presenter: Lesson 3: **Learning new skills**
A Listen and tick the words you hear. If you get three ticks in a line, say Bingo!
[REPEAT OF LESSON 2 EXERCISE C]

Presenter: **B 2 Listen and check your answers.**
Voice: pay – letter p
Bill – letter b
Penn – letter p
personal – letter p
Bean – letter b
Peter – letter p
people – letter p
place – letter p
pleased – letter p

Beale – letter b
Polly – letter p
principal – letter p
problems – letter p
behind – letter b

Presenter: **B** **3** **Listen to these words connected with education. Is the missing letter _p_ or _b_?**

Voice:
a book
b paper
c begin
d spell
e pass
f period
g subject
h explain

Presenter: **C** **2** **Look at these pairs of words. Listen. Which do you hear in each case? Don't worry about the meanings.**

Voice:
a hill
b steal
c will
d meal
e pill
f kill
g feel
h feet
i Bill
j beat

Presenter: **D** **Listen to the first part of the principal's speech again. It's much slower this time.**
Put your left hand up every time you hear _p_.
Put your right hand up every time you hear _b_.

Peter Bean: OK. Let's begin. Welcome to Greenhill College. I am very pleased to see you all here.
My name is Peter Bean. I'm the principal. You come and see me if you have any problems with the fees – that means the money you must pay. My office is on the first floor, Room 15, by the stairs. The people behind me are some of my staff. This is Mrs Polly Penn. She's the head of Year 1. She is responsible for the schedule. After this meeting, Mrs Penn will give you the schedule for the first term. The schedule tells you the times of all your lectures.

Presenter: **E** **Listen to the second part of the speech again.**
Say _i_ every time you hear the short sound.
Say _ee_ every time you hear the long sound.

Peter Bean: Mrs Penn will also give you the name of your instructor. We call the teachers at Greenhill instructors. She will also tell you the name of your personal advisor – that's a person who helps you if you have problems. Finally, this is the registrar, Mr Bill Beale. He's in charge of attendance. If you can't come to the college one day, tell Mr Beale. OK, that's it from me. Now I'll hand over to Mrs Penn … Oh, I nearly forgot. Mr Beale's room is on the first floor, next to my room – Room 16.

Presenter: **Lesson 4: Applying new skills**
B **Listen to some sentences from the principal's speech in Lesson 2. What is Mrs Penn going to talk about? Tick one or more topic.**

Peter Bean: This is Mrs Polly Penn. She's the head of Year 1. She is responsible for the schedule. After this meeting, Mrs Penn will give you the schedule for the first term. The schedule tells you the times of all your lectures. Mrs Penn will also give you the name of your instructor.

We call the teachers at Greenhill instructors. She will also tell you the name of your personal advisor – that's a person who helps you if you have problems.

Presenter: **C** **Listen to Mrs Penn's speech. Underline the topics to check your answers to Exercise B.**

Polly Penn: OK. First, your schedule. In the first term, you do General Studies and English. General Studies means subjects like religion, maths, science and the arts. So, every day, you do three periods of General Studies in the morning and three of English in the afternoon.
If you have any problems with any of your studies, go and see your personal advisor. The advisors' rooms are on the third floor. Now, listen carefully.
If your surname – I mean your family name – begins with A, B, C, D or E, your advisor is Mrs Piper.
If your surname begins with F, G, H, I or J, your advisor is Mrs Barber.
If your surname begins with K, L, M, N or O, your advisor is Mrs Peebles.
If your surname begins with P, Q, R, S or T, your advisor is Mrs Bream.
If your surname begins with U, V, W, X, Y or Z, your advisor is Mrs Pinner.

Presenter: **D** **Imagine you are a new student at Greenhill College.**
1 **Listen to the first part of Mrs Penn's speech again. Which schedule above is correct for you?**

Polly Penn: OK. First, your schedule. In the first term, you do General Studies and English. General Studies means subjects like religion, maths, science and the arts. So, every day, you do three periods of General Studies in the morning and three of English in the afternoon.

Presenter: **2** **Listen to the second part of Mrs Penn's speech again. What is the name of your personal advisor? Tick one.**

Polly Penn: If you have any problems with any of your studies, go and see your personal advisor. The advisors' rooms are on the third floor. Now, listen carefully.
If your surname – I mean your family name – begins with A, B, C, D or E, your advisor is Mrs Piper.
If your surname begins with F, G, H, I or J, your advisor is Mrs Barber.
If your surname begins with K, L, M, N or O, your advisor is Mrs Peebles.
If your surname begins with P, Q, R, S or T, your advisor is Mrs Bream.
If your surname begins with U, V, W, X, Y or Z, your advisor is Mrs Pinner.

Presenter: **Theme 2: Daily Life, Schedules**
Lesson 1: Vocabulary
C **Listen to some sentences with the green words. Number the words in order.**

Voice:
1 There is a very good restaurant in North Road. The food is excellent.
2 I don't like chess. In fact, I don't like any games like that.
3 Do you play any sports? Football, basketball, handball?
4 My sister is excellent at music. She plays the piano, the flute and the guitar.
5 Have you joined the college computer club yet?
6 This university has a very big campus – there are about twenty college buildings and several houses for students to live in.
7 It is very important to plan your day. Make sure

there is time for college work and family life.

8   I watched the new Indian film at the cinema yesterday.

Presenter: Lesson 2: Listening
  C   Listen to Mrs Penn's definitions and check your answers.
Mrs Penn: a   I'm going to give you your schedule – that's the days and times of your classes – for this semester, OK?
  b   First I want you to write the start time and the end time of each period – in other words, each part of the day.
  c   Lunch is served in the cafeteria – that's the restaurant on the campus.
  d   You have a short recess – I mean, a short break between classes.

Presenter: **D   Mrs Penn is going to give you your schedule. Listen and answer these questions.**
Mrs Penn: OK. Is everybody ready? Have you all got a pencil? Good. I'm going to give you your schedule – that's the days and times of your classes – for this semester, OK? Can you fill it in as I read it out? If you're not sure about anything, ask your friends after this talk. OK. First I want you to write the start time and the end time of each period – in other words, each part of the day. As you can see, there are six periods, three in the morning and three in the afternoon. There's also a lunch period which lasts an hour. Lunch is served in the cafeteria – that's the restaurant on the campus. OK. Each period is one hour, so that's three hours in the morning and … how many hours in the afternoon?
Student 1: Three.
Mrs Penn: Good. The first period begins at 9 o'clock. So can you write 9 o'clock in the first morning space? When does the first period end?
Student 2: Half past nine.
Mrs Penn: No, not half past nine.
Student 3: 9.45?
Mrs Penn: No! Come on, think!
Student 1: 10 o'clock.
Mrs Penn: Why?
Student 1: Because each period is one hour.
Mrs Penn: Right. Good. So the next period begins at 10 o'clock, right?
Student 1: Yes.
Mrs Penn: Wrong. You have a short recess – I mean, a short break between classes. The recess is 10 minutes long. So the next period begins at …?
Student 2: Five past ten.
Student 3: Ten past ten.
Mrs Penn: That's right. OK. So now you can fill in the other times …

Presenter: **E   Listen again.**
  [REPEAT OF LESSON 2 EXERCISE D]

Presenter: **F   2   Listen and check your ideas.**
Voice: a   each   column 2
  b   give   column 1
  c   mean   column 2
  d   read   column 2
  e   see   column 2
  f   six   column 1
  g   this   column 1
  h   three   column 2
  i   begins   column 1
  j   between   column 2

Presenter: **G   2   Listen and check your ideas.**
Voice: a   about   letter b
  b   because   letter b
  c   begins   letter b
  d   pencil   letter p
  e   between   letter b
  f   break   letter b
  g   space   letter p
  h   campus   letter p
  i   part   letter p
  j   period   letter p

Presenter: Lesson 3: Learning new skills
  B   1   Listen to eight times. Letter the clocks A to H.
Voice: c   six o'clock
  f   ten past eight
  b   quarter past seven
  d   twenty past four
  g   half past eleven
  a   twenty to ten
  h   quarter to three
  e   It's ten to four.

Presenter: **3   Listen to the times again and check.**
  [REPEAT OF LESSON 3 EXERCISE B1]

Presenter: **C   3   Listen and check your ideas.**
Mrs Penn: a   Have you all got a pencil?
  b   ask your friends
  c   after this talk
  d   the start time
  e   each part of the day
  f   in the afternoon
  g   it lasts an hour
  h   in the cafeteria
  i   on the campus
  j   half past nine

Presenter: Lesson 4: Applying new skills
  C   Mrs Penn runs the extracurricular activities at Greenhill College. Listen and find out:
  1   the meaning of extracurricular;
  2   the extracurricular activities at the college – tick the activities on the notice board.
Mrs Penn: OK, so that's the schedule. Now, some other information for you. We have extracurricular activities – that means extra things you can do after college work every evening, so can you make a note of these? If you want to do any of the activities, just come along to the first meeting this week.
  Right. First, we have Sports Club on Saturday at 8 o'clock in the evening – you can do basketball, handball, table tennis and lots of other sports.
  Then there's Film Night on Sunday, starting at 8.30. We have a different film every week and after the film, there's a discussion.
  It's Quiz Time on Monday. Come with a friend and take part in a General Knowledge quiz. That starts at quarter to eight.
  Computer Club is on Tuesday. It doesn't matter whether you are a beginner or an expert. Come and learn or just have fun. Computer Club starts at quarter past eight.
  Finally, we have Music Makers on Wednesday night. If you play an instrument or want to learn, join the music makers at half past seven. I'll run through those again in case you missed anything.

Presenter:	**D Listen again and write in the days and times for each activity that you ticked.**
	[REPEAT OF LESSON 4 EXERCISE C]

Presenter:	**Theme 3: Work and Business, Work Starts Now!**
	Lesson 1: Vocabulary
	B Listen to some sentences with the green words. Then complete each sentence.

Voice:
1 People don't like him at work. They can't rely on him. They never know if he will be late, or not come to work at all.
2 It is very important to have good colleagues to work with in a job.
3 That work isn't urgent. You can do it tomorrow.
4 Where are the papers for my next meeting? Are they in the file?
5 If you are paid every month, we call that money salary.
6 Some companies make products – real things like computers, televisions or cars.
7 Some companies give services –– like banks, cleaning companies or car hire companies.

Presenter:	**Lesson 2: Listening**
	B Gerald Gardiner is a management consultant. He is at Greenhill College today. He is talking to the first-year students about work. Listen to the first part of his talk.
	1 How many points does he make?
	2 Can you remember any of the points?

Gerald Gardiner:
How do you get a good job when you leave college? You start thinking about it NOW! Change the way that you think about college. Think of college as a job – your job. You will find it much easier then to live in the world of work in two or three years' time.
So college should be a job. But what is a job? What must you do in a job? I'm going to tell you nine things.
Number 1: You must go to work every day.
Number 2: You must be punctual – that means, you must always be on time.
Number 3: You must respect your manager – the person who gives you orders – and your colleagues – that is, the people you work with.
Number 4: You must also respect the customers, in other words, the people who buy things from the company.
Number 5: You must do all the tasks or pieces of work that your manager gives you.
Number 6: You must complete all your tasks on time.
Number 7: You are responsible for the quality of your work – whether it is good or bad.
Number 8: You must keep your workplace tidy – your desk, and any shelves or cupboards that you use.
Number 9: You must organise your work files sensibly – in alphabetical order or chronologically – in other words, by date.

Presenter:	**C Listen again. How does he define these words? Match each word to a definition.**
	[REPEAT OF LESSON 1 EXERCISE B]

Presenter:	**E Listen again and check your answers.**
	[REPEAT OF LESSON 1 EXERCISE B]

Presenter:	**F 2 Listen and check your ideas.**

Voice:
are	column D
bad	column C
colleagues	column B
gives	column A
keep	column B
leave	column B
manager	column C
people	column B
pieces	column B
start	column D
that	column C
think	column A

Presenter:	**G 2 Listen and check your ideas.**

Voice:
a	punctual	letter p
b	respect	letter p
c	buy	letter b
d	pieces	letter p
e	sensibly	letter b
f	people	letter p
g	job	letter b
h	company	letter p
i	responsible	letter p
j	workplace	letter p
k	complete	letter p
l	person	letter p

Presenter:	**Lesson 3: Learning new skills**
	B 2 Listen and check your ideas.

Voice:
a You must go to work every day.
b You must be punctual.
c You must respect your manager and your colleagues.
d You must also respect the customers.
e You must do all the tasks or pieces of work that your manager gives you.
f You must complete all your tasks on time.
g You are responsible for the quality of your work.
h You must keep your workplace tidy.
i You must organise your work files sensibly.

Presenter:	**C 2 Listen and check your answers.**

Voice:
go	row A
give	row A
college	row B
get	row A
change	row B
colleague	row A
organise	row A

Presenter:	**4 Listen and check your answers.**

Voice:
age	row B
page	row B
begin	row A
charge	row B
ago	row A
again	row A
large	row B
big	row A

Presenter:	**6 Listen and check your answers.**

Voice:
danger	row B
angry	row A
wage	row B
magazine	row A
rig	row A

Presenter:	**Lesson 4: Applying new skills**
	D 1 Listen and write one or two stressed words under *Gerald's reasons* in the blue table. Guess the spelling.

Gerald Gardiner:
Why must you do all these things in a job? Let's look at each thing and suggest a reason.
You must go to work every day. Why? Because people

rely on you. They need you to do your work so they can do their work.

You must be punctual. Why? Because people expect you at a certain time. If you are late, you waste their time. You must respect your manager and your colleagues. Why? Because you have to work together every day. You must respect the customers. Why? Because, in the end, they pay your wages.

You must do all the tasks that your manager gives you. Why? Because all jobs have interesting tasks and boring tasks, easy tasks and difficult tasks.

You must complete all your tasks on time. Why? Because other people need the information.

You are responsible for the quality of your work. Why? Because it is very bad for a company if a customer is dissatisfied with a product or service.

You must keep your workplace tidy. Why? Because it is rude to make other people put up with your mess.

You must organise your work files sensibly. Why? Because you might be ill one day. Then a manager or colleague will have to find urgent papers in your work files.

Presenter: **2 Listen again. Make notes on Gerald's reasons where you have a cross. Listen for the important words.**
[REPEAT OF LESSON 4 EXERCISE D]

Presenter: **Theme 4: Science and Nature, So You Want to Be a Scientist?**
Lesson 1: Vocabulary
C Listen to a paragraph. Then write one of the green words in each space.

Voice: Science is the study of how things work in the world. A scientist usually works in a laboratory. He or she tests things to find out the facts. He or she often puts the facts in a table, with columns of information, or in a graph, with blocks or lines that represent the information.

Presenter: **Lesson 2: Listening**
C 1 Listen to the introduction to the programme. Tick each point in the programme information when Arthur mentions it.

Arthur Burns: This week on *So you want to be...* we are looking at the job of the scientist. What is science? What do scientists do? What is scientific method? And the most important question of all: Is science the right career for you?

Presenter: **2 Listen to the first part of the programme. Put your hand up when Arthur starts to talk about a new point.**

Arthur Burns: First, what is science? Science is the study of how things work in the world. The word *science* comes from Greek and Latin words meaning 'to know'. What do scientists do? Well, scientists are not satisfied just to *think* something is true. They must *prove* it. *Proving* means showing that something is always true. In this way, scientists are different from other people. Let me show you the difference.

I know that plants need sunlight and water to live. At least, I think that's true. But thinking is not enough for a scientist. If a scientist *thinks* something is true, he or she wants to *prove* it.

How can scientists prove that something is true? They must follow the scientific method. A method is a way of doing something. But what is the scientific method? It works like this: Firstly, a scientist makes a hypothesis, which means an idea of the truth. Then he or she tests

the hypothesis. Scientists can test hypotheses in two main ways. They can do an experiment, which means a test in a laboratory. Scientists study what happens during the experiment. Or they can do research, which means looking up information. They usually do research in a library or, nowadays, on the Internet. With research, scientists look at what happened in the past.

In both cases – experiments and research – they collect data. Data is information before it is organised. Then they display the results in a table or a graph. Then they draw conclusions. Conclusions are what you learn from an experiment. The hypothesis is proved – or disproved. Does this sound interesting to you? Is science the right career for you?

Presenter: **D Listen again. How does Arthur Burns define these words?**
[REPEAT OF LESSON 2 EXERCISE C2]

Presenter: **E Look at the student notes on the right. Listen to the first part of the programme again. Complete the notes by writing one word in each space.**
[REPEAT OF LESSON 2 EXERCISE C2]

Presenter: **F 2 Listen and check your ideas.**
Voice:

display	column A
even	column B
enough	column A
graph	column D
Greek	column B
happen	column C
if	column A
lab	column C
past	column D
plant	column D

Presenter: **G 2 Listen and check your ideas.**
Voice:

a	prove	letter p
b	display	letter p
c	both	letter b
d	table	letter b
e	past	letter p
f	disprove	letter p
g	hypothesis	letter p
h	experiment	letter p
i	lab	letter b
j	happen	letter p

Presenter: **Lesson 3: Learning new skills**
C 2 Listen to some of Arthur's sentences. Choose the next word from the yellow box each time Arthur pauses. Write the number beside the word.

Arthur Burns: 1 Science is the study of how things work in the [PAUSE] world. Science is the study of how things work in the world.

2 The word 'science' comes from Greek and Latin words meaning to [PAUSE] *know*. The word 'science' comes from Greek and Latin words meaning to *know*.

3 Scientists must prove that something is [PAUSE] true. Scientists must prove that something is true.

4 They must follow the scientific [PAUSE] method. They must follow the scientific method.

5 Scientists must collect [PAUSE] data. Scientists must collect data.

6 They display the results in a table or [PAUSE] graph. They display the results in a table or graph.

Presenter: **D 2 Listen and check your answers.**

Voice:		
	that	column B
	the	column B
	they	column B
	both	column A
	then	column B
	there	column B
	hypothesis	column A
	with	column B
	thing	column A
	truth	column A

Presenter: **E 2 Listen and check your answers.**

Voice: test   when   then   pen   she   bed   many   any   head   again

Presenter: **Lesson 4: Applying new skills**
B Listen to the next part of the programme with Arthur Burns. What does Arthur ask you to do? Make a sentence with these groups of words.

Arthur Burns: At the beginning of the programme, I said: I think plants need sunlight and water to live. But a scientist isn't satisfied with *think*. He or she wants to *know*. How can I *prove* that plants need sunlight and water to live? Can you think of an experiment to prove this hypothesis? I'll be back after these messages.

Presenter: **D Listen to the next part of the programme. When Arthur stops speaking, say the next word.**

Arthur Burns: Welcome back. Well, did you think of an [PAUSE] experiment?
If you did, perhaps a career in science is right for you. If you didn't … well, perhaps you would like to hear about my [PAUSE] experiment.
Remember: my hypothesis was that plants need sunlight and water to live.
The experiment: I bought three plants of the same type.
I put each plant into a [PAUSE] pot. The pots were all the same size.
I filled each pot with the same kind of [PAUSE] soil.
I put each plant pot on a [PAUSE] saucer.
I put all three plants outside.
I covered Plant 1 with black plastic. So Plant 1 did not have any [PAUSE] sunlight.
I watered Plant 1 and Plant 3 for one week but I did not give Plant 2 any [PAUSE] water.
What result did I get?
Remember: Plant 1 did not have any sunlight.
It was yellow and very [PAUSE] small.
Plant 2 did not have any water.
It was [PAUSE] dead.
Plant 3 had sunlight and water.
It was green and very [PAUSE] healthy.
My conclusion is: Plants need sunlight and water to live.
I have proved my hypothesis.
Have I proved that science is a good career for you?

Presenter: **Theme 5: The Physical World, Where Is Your Country?**
Lesson 1: Vocabulary
C Listen to descriptions of six countries. Look at the map. Find each country.

Voice:
1 It is in North America. It is north of the USA.
2 It is in Asia. It is south-east of Pakistan.
3 It is in Africa. It is west of Egypt.
4 It is in Europe. It is west of Spain.
5 It is in Australasia. It is a large island. It is on the Tropic of Capricorn. It is near New Zealand.
6 It is in South America. It is between the Equator and the Tropic of Capricorn. It is north of Argentina.

Presenter: **Lesson 2: Listening**
B 1 Listen. Donna pauses a few times in her questions. Guess the word she is going to say next on each occasion. Listen and check your ideas.

Donna: Where are you [PAUSE] from, Fatma?
Fatma: I'm from Kuwait.
Donna: Where's [PAUSE] that?
Fatma: It's in the north of the Gulf. It's north-east of Saudi Arabia.
Donna: And where do you come [PAUSE] from in Kuwait?
Fatma: I come from Al Khiran.
Donna: How do you spell [PAUSE] that?
Fatma: A-L K-H-I-R-A-N.
Donna: Which part of the [PAUSE] country is that in?
Fatma: Well, Kuwait is very small, but it's in the south-east.
Donna: Is Al Khiran the capital?
Fatma: No. The capital is Kuwait City.
Donna: What about you, Fairuza?
Fairuza: I'm from Oman.
Donna: Is that in the Gulf, [PAUSE] too?
Fairuza: Yes, well, not exactly. It's south-west of the UAE and Saudi Arabia.
Donna: Does it have a long coastline?
Fairuza: Yes, that's right. It has a coastline on the Arabian Sea.
Donna: And what's your home [PAUSE] town?
Fairuza: I'm from Salalah.
Donna: Sorry. What did you [PAUSE] say?
Fairuza: I said, Salalah.
Donna: How do you spell [PAUSE] that?
Fairuza: S-A-L-A-L-A-H.
Donna: Is that the [PAUSE] capital?
Fairuza: No, the capital is Muscat.
Donna: Which part of the country is Salalah [PAUSE] in?
Fairuza: It's in the south.

Presenter: **B 3 Listen again. Complete the information about Kuwait and Oman.**
[REPEAT OF LESSON 2 EXERCISE B1 WITHOUT PAUSES]

Presenter: **D 2 Listen and check your ideas.**

Voice:		
	city	columns A and B
	did	column A
	east	column B
	exactly	columns A, C and B
	Oman	column D
	said	column E
	Salalah	column D
	spell	column E
	west	column E

Presenter: **E 2 Listen and check your ideas.**

Voice:		
	a about	letter b
	b capital	letter p
	c north	letters t and h
	d part	letter p
	e south	letters t and h
	f spell	letter p

Presenter: F **Listen and complete these words from earlier themes.**

Voice:
1 college
2 display
3 experiment
4 job
5 manager
6 method
7 past
8 prove
9 think
10 punctual

Presenter: **Lesson 3: Learning new skills**
B 3 **Listen and put the other letters of the alphabet into the correct column, according to the vowel sound.**

Voice: A B C D E F G H I J K L M N O P Q R S T U V W X Y Z

Presenter: C 1 **Listen to the spellings on the cassette. Write the letters and find out the words.**

Voice:
1 U-K
2 U-A-E
3 U-S-A
4 O-M-A-N
5 Q-A-T-A-R
6 K-U-W-A-I-T
7 B-A-H-R-A-I-N
8 Y-E-M-E-N
9 J-A-P-A-N
10 C-H-I-N-A
11 S-A-U-D-I A-R-A-B-I-A
12 G-U-L-F

Presenter: D 3 **Listen and check your ideas.**

Voice: it's is small south has east coast what's sorry does spell say towns

Presenter: E 4 **Listen to the words in Exercises 1 and 2.**

Voice: Exercise 1: on not from what come of sorry want was wash
Exercise 2: for before more small talk war August taught north

Presenter: **Lesson 4: Applying new skills**
B 2 **Listen and tick the topics you hear.**

Lecturer: The Sultanate of Oman is situated north of the Equator.
The capital city, Muscat, which in English is spelt M-U-S-C-A-T, is on the Tropic of Cancer – that's Tropic, T-R-O-P-I-C, of Cancer, C-A-N-C-E-R.
Oman is bordered to the north-west by the UAE and to the north-east by the Gulf of Oman.
To the west, there is a long, undefined border with Saudi Arabia, while to the south-east, Oman has a long coastline on the Arabian Sea.
In the south-west, there is a border with Yemen – Y-E-M-E-N.
There is also a small area in the far north that belongs to Oman. It is called Musandam – M-U-S-A-N-D-A-M. The total area of the country is 212,500 square kilometres. This is about three times the area of the UAE.
The country consists of stony desert, with a sandy desert in the south-east called Wahiba Sands – that's W-A-H-I-B-A. The border with Saudi Arabia is also sand desert. This is the famous Rub al Khali, or Empty Quarter.

There are mountains in the centre of the country – Jebel Akhdar – J-E-B-E-L A-K-H-D-A-R. There are also mountains in the north – the Hajar – H-A-J-A-R.

Presenter: 3 **Listen again and label the map.**
[REPEAT OF LESSON 4 EXERCISE B2]

Presenter: **Theme 6: Culture and Civilization, Congratulations!**
Lesson 1: Vocabulary
C **Listen to a paragraph. Then write one of the green words in each space.**

Voice: In some parts of Pakistan there are traditional events for children. The first event is called *Bismillah Khawni*. It takes place when the child is four years and four months. The boy or girl wears special clothes with flowers on, and family and friends watch him or her say the first chapter of the *Holy Qur'an*. The celebration ends with a special dinner. The second event is called *Khtme Qur'an*. This event celebrates the child's ability to say the complete *Holy Qur'an*. The child receives gifts and, once again, there is a special dinner.

Presenter: **Lesson 2: Listening**
B **Listen to the talk once.**
1 **Juri pauses a few times during her talk. Guess the word that she is going to say next. Listen and check your ideas.**

Juri: I'm going to talk to you today about a festival in Japan. The festival is called *Seijin-no-hi*, which is spelt S-E-I-J-I-N N-O H-I. The name means the Coming of Age festival. This festival is for all girls and [PAUSE] boys who become 20 years old in that year. It takes place on the second Monday of January each year. The festival celebrates the change from being a child to being an [PAUSE] adult. At the age of 20, a person in Japan can vote and smoke! There is a ceremony in a town hall. Town halls – H-A-L-L-S – are the local government offices. First, government officials make speeches. Then they give small presents to the new [PAUSE] adults. Young women wear traditional dresses called kimonos. The word is spelt [PAUSE] K-I-M-O-N-O. They usually rent the kimonos, because they can cost as much as a [PAUSE] car. Young men wear business suits or, occasionally, dark kimonos. Later, after the ceremony, the new adults go to special [PAUSE] parties. Finally, the young people go [PAUSE] home. They go out in the morning as children. They come back in the evening as [PAUSE] adults.

Presenter: C 2 **Listen to the talk again, without the pauses. Make notes in the table below.**
[REPEAT OF LESSON 2 EXERCISE B1 WITHOUT PAUSES]

Presenter: E 2 **Listen and check your answers.**

Voice:

after	column A
all	column B
although	column B
called	column B
dark	column A
first	column C
girl	column C
hall	column B
or	column B
parties	column A
person	column C
small	column B

Presenter: **F What are the missing letters in each of these sentences? Listen and write the letters.**

Juri:
1 I'm going to talk to you about the Coming of Age festival.
2 It takes place on the second Monday of January.
3 It celebrates the change from being a child to being an adult.
4 Town halls are local government offices.
5 First, officials make speeches.
6 Then they give small presents.
7 Young women wear traditional dresses.
8 They usually rent the kimonos.
9 They can cost as much as a car.

Presenter: **Lesson 3: Learning new skills**
B 3 Listen and check.

Juri: I'm going to talk to you today about a festival in Japan.
First, government officials make speeches.
Then they give small presents to the new adults.
Later, after the ceremony, the new adults go to special parties.
Finally, the young people go home.

Presenter: **C 1 Listen to the words in the blue box. Which consonant is missing in each case?**

Voice: talk
take
twenty
vote
festival
party
after
later

Presenter: **2 Listen to the words in the yellow box. Which consonant is missing in each case?**

Voice: dark
adult
traditional
dinner
day
idea
die
understand

Presenter: **Lesson 4: Applying new skills**
C 1 Listen to the first part. Make notes to answer the first seven questions.

Adriana: I'm going to talk to you this morning about a festival in Mexico. It is called Quinceañera, spelt Q-U-I-N-C-E-A-N-E-R-A. The name means *fifteen years*. The festival is for girls. It happens when a girl becomes 15 years old. It is a coming of age celebration. In the past in Mexico, parents expected a daughter to get married after she was 15, but today it just means the child has become an adult. The girl usually wears a long pink or white dress.

Presenter: **2 Listen to the second part. Complete the information about the events in order.**

Adriana: On the girl's 15th birthday, there are several special events. First, the girl's family and friends go to a ceremony in a church. There are speeches in the church. Then, fourteen couples walk with the birthday girl – one couple for each year of her life. After that, the girl gives a small doll to her younger sister. Finally, after the ceremony, there is a party in a local hall, or at the home of the girl's parents.

Presenter: **Theme 7: They Made Our World, Who? What? When?**
Lesson 1: Vocabulary
C Listen to a paragraph. Then write one of the green words or phrases in each space. Make any necessary changes.

Voice: Nowadays, we can travel in many different ways. On land, we can ride on a bicycle or drive in a car. In many countries, we can also go along special tracks in a train. On the sea, we can sail in a small boat or cruise in a large ship. In the air, we can fly in a small plane or in a huge one. How did we get all these forms of transport? Who invented them? When did each invention happen?

Presenter: **Lesson 2: Listening**
B 1 What is the lecturer going to talk about? Look at the notebook. Listen and number the points in order.

Lecturer: I'm going to talk to you today about inventions; that is, new ways of doing something. All the inventions are in the field, or area, of transport. First, I'm going to talk about different methods or types of transport. After that, I'll tell you when each method was invented. Finally, I'm going to say which invention was the most important, as far as I am concerned – I mean, in my opinion.

Presenter: **2 Listen again and check your answers.**
[REPEAT OF LESSON 2 EXERCISE B1]

Presenter: **3 Listen to the second part. When the lecturer stops, guess the next word. Then check your guesses.**

Lecturer: OK. So, first, what are the main methods of transport that we use today?
We can travel on land, on the sea and in the [PAUSE] air. We use cars and bicycles, trains, boats and, of course, [PAUSE] planes.
OK. So, there are several methods of [PAUSE] transport. But when was each method [PAUSE] invented?

Presenter: **4 Copy Table 1. Then listen to the third part and complete the table.**

Lecturer: The first method of transport was of course, *walking*. But about 40,000 years ago – yes, that's right, 40,000 – some Indonesian natives made a boat and sailed from one island to another. For centuries, man sailed the seas using only the power of the wind. Then, in 1775, J.C. Perier – that's P-E-R-I-E-R – invented the steamship. Steam also powered the first train. In 1830, George Stephenson, which is spelt S-T-E-P-H-E-N-S-O-N, drove his engine, called the *Rocket*, along a track, and the Railway Age began. Just nine years later, in 1839, a man called Macmillan, spelt M-A-C-M-I-L-L-A-N, invented the bicycle. Fifty years after that, in 1888, Karl Benz – that's B-E-N-Z – invented the motor car. So now man could move quickly on land and on the sea. Finally, at the beginning of the 20th century, in 1903, the Wright Brothers conquered the air. That's Wright with a silent W – W-R-I-G-H-T. Their plane, called *Flyer*, flew a distance of 35 metres and went down in history.

Presenter: **5 Listen to the final part.**
Lecturer: So we have heard about the main inventions in the field of transport. But which invention was the most important? In my opinion, it was the last invention, the plane. This invention has made the world into a much smaller place. People can travel right to the

other side of the world in a day. Why is that important? Because the more we travel, the more we understand other people and other cultures.

Presenter: C Listen to the third part of the lecture again. Complete Table 1 with dates and names.
[REPEAT OF LESSON 2 EXERCISE B4]

Presenter: D 2 Listen and check your answers.
Voice: Column A. ship which wind history engine
Column B. land track transport that
Column C. tell when went engine
Column D. on was what because

Presenter: E 2 Listen and check your answers.
Voice: Column A. sea steam each people
Column B. car after last far
Column C. first world concerned
Column D. talk course transport called more walk
Column E. new flew move use

Presenter: Lesson 3: Learning new skills
B 2 Listen to the introduction again and check your answer.
[REPEAT OF LESSON 2 EXERCISE B1]

Presenter: D 2 Listen and check your ideas.
Voice: a check
b each
c English
d match
e much
f ship
g short
h which

Presenter: Lesson 4: Applying new skills
B 2 Listen to the introduction. Correct Vicente's work.
Lecturer: I'm going to talk to you today about inventions. All the inventions are in the field of flying. First, I'm going to talk about different methods of flying. After that, I'll tell you when each method was invented and who invented it. Finally, I'm going to say which invention was the most important, in my opinion.

Presenter: C Listen to the second part of the lecture. When the lecturer stops, guess the next word. Then check your guesses.
Lecturer: OK. So, first, what are the main methods of flying that we use today? There is the plane itself, then the jet plane, which is much [PAUSE] faster. For transporting large numbers of people, there is the jumbo jet. The jumbo jet can carry more than 500 [PAUSE] people. A very different kind of flying machine is the helicopter. It can go straight up and straight [PAUSE] down. It can even stay in one place. Finally, there is the rocket that takes astronauts into [PAUSE] space. And of course, the space [PAUSE] shuttle, which takes them up into space and brings them [PAUSE] back.

Presenter: D Listen to the third part of the lecture. How does the lecturer define these words?
Lecturer: OK. So, there are several methods of flying. But when was each method invented? And who invented it? The Wright brothers flew the first plane with an engine in 1903. The plane had two propellers – pieces of wood that turn to pull the plane through the air. For nearly 30 years, the propeller plane was the only type, but in 1930, Frank Whittle – spelt W-H-I-T-T-L-E – invented the jet engine. Jet means a very fast stream of something – in this case, air. Jet planes can go much faster than propeller planes. In 1970, the American aircraft company, Boeing – that's B-O-E-I-N-G – invented the jumbo jet. Jumbo means very big. Much earlier, in around 1910, Sikorsky built the first successful helicopter. Sixteen years later, in 1926, Robert Goddard invented the rocket, but it was not until 1961 that Russian scientists sent a man into space in a rocket. Finally, in 1976, NASA – N-A-S-A – which is the American space administration, invented a plane that could go into space and return to Earth. They called it the space shuttle. A shuttle is something that goes to a place and comes back.

Presenter: E Listen to the third part again. Complete Table 1 with inventions, dates and names.
[REPEAT OF LESSON 4 EXERCISE D]

Presenter: F Listen to the final part.
Lecturer: So we have heard about the main inventions in the field of flying. But which invention was the most important? In my opinion, it was the last invention, the space shuttle. This invention has helped us to reach out into space. From space, we see the world as it really is – a small ball that we must look after.

Presenter: Theme 8: Art and Literature, There Was Once a Poor Man …
Lesson 1: Vocabulary
B 3 Listen and check your ideas.
Voice: Column A. checked looked stopped talked walked
Column B. carried climbed moved lived
Column C. ended pointed started wanted

Presenter: C 2 Listen to 15 irregular past tense verbs. Write the number of the past tense verb you hear next to the correct infinitive in the list of red words.
Voice: 1 said
2 came
3 found
4 left
5 gave
6 told
7 took
8 met
9 got
10 went
11 put
12 sent
13 ran
14 brought
15 built

Presenter: D Listen to a paragraph. Then write one of the green words in each space.
Voice: Everybody likes a good story. There are stories in the literature of every culture. Children learn them at home or at school. Many of these stories have a moral – in other words, a lesson for life. For example, help people and they will help you. There is usually one main character – one person who does most of the actions. We often don't know the name of the writer of these traditional stories. People often translate the best stories into many languages so, in the end, the same story appears all around the world.

Presenter: Lesson 2: Listening
C 2 Listen to the first part of the programme and check your answers.

Jenny Ingram: In this programme, we're going to hear about *The Arabian Nights*. First, I'm going to talk about the history of the stories. After that, we're going to listen to one of the stories.

So first, the history. *The Arabian Nights*, or *The Thousand and One Nights*, is a collection of stories from Persia, Arabia, India and Egypt. The stories are anonymous – in other words, nobody knows who made up the stories, who wrote them. For centuries, they have been part of the folklore – that means, the traditional stories passed, by word of mouth, from generation to generation, from father to son and mother to daughter. A few of the stories appeared around AD800. Then, in around 1500, an unknown Egyptian wrote down the stories that we know today. This collection included stories of Aladdin – the boy who found a wonderful lamp, Sindbad the sailor, who met a fabulous bird, the Roc, and Ali Baba and his problems with the Forty Thieves. The stories were translated from Arabic into French in 1717. The person who translated them was a Frenchman and his name was Galland – that's G-A-L-L-A-N-D. Later, in 1885, they were translated from Arabic into English. This translation was by the English explorer Sir Richard Burton. His surname is spelt B-U-R-T-O-N.

The Arabian Nights is the most widely known piece of Arabic literature in the Western World.

Presenter: **D Listen again. Complete the table.**
[REPEAT OF LESSON 2 EXERCISE C2]

Presenter: **F Listen to the story. Which sentence about the story is true?**

Jenny Ingram: Here is one of the stories from *The Arabian Nights*. It is called *The Thieves and the Donkey*.

There were once two thieves, a young man and an old man. They were at a market. They saw a poor man buy a donkey. The poor man put a rope around the donkey's neck and led the donkey away from the market.
'We can steal that donkey easily,' the young thief said to the old thief.
The young thief went up behind the poor man and untied the rope from the donkey. He put the rope around his own neck. The old thief took the donkey away.
The young thief walked behind the poor man for some time. Suddenly, the young thief stopped and the poor man looked round. He was very surprised to see a man at the end of the rope, not the donkey.
'Who are you?' he asked. 'And where's my donkey?'
'I *am* your donkey,' the young thief said. 'I was rude to my mother and, suddenly, I became a donkey. I was a donkey for several years and then you bought me. Just now, I became a man again.'
The man untied the rope from the young thief's neck.
'Go back to your home. And do not be rude to your mother again.'
The poor man still wanted a donkey, so he went back to the market the next day. He was surprised to see his donkey for sale again. He went up to the donkey and said:
'I told you not to be rude to your mother again.'

Presenter: **G 1 Listen to the words in Column A.**
Voice: lived
means
led
words
man
passed
not
called
young
rude
took

Presenter: **2 Listen to the words in the orange box. Write each word in a space in Column B.**
Voice: back
bought
his
looked
market
mother
problem
thief
went
who
world

Presenter: **3 Write each word from the yellow box in a space in Column C. Listen and check.**
Voice: English
steal
said
bird
lamp
father
stopped
story
son
few
put

Presenter: Lesson 3: Learning new skills
C Who did what? Listen to the story in Lesson 2 again. Answer each question with 1, 2 or 3.
[REPEAT OF LESSON 2 EXERCISE F]

Presenter: **D Look at these words from the talk. Listen. Tick the correct column, according to the stressed vowel sound.**
Voice: away
became
behind
buy
eighty
famous
generation
made
tie
time
translate

Presenter: Lesson 4: Applying new skills
B Listen to the first part of the programme. Complete the table.

Jenny Ingram: There are stories about a wise fool in the folklore of many countries. A wise fool is a person who does silly things but has a clever reason for them.
In Greece, he is Chotzas – C-H-O-T-Z-A-S.
In China, he is called Afandi – A-F-A-N-D-I.

In Turkey, he is called Hodja – H-O-D-J-A – or Nasreddin – N-A-S-R-E-D-D-I-N.
The stories first appeared in these countries hundreds of years ago. But was Hodja ever a real person? The Turks say 'Yes'. They say he was born in 1208 and died in 1284. But there were stories in the Arab World in around AD 750 about a character called Joha – J-O-H-A – or Goha – G-O-H-A. Did the name *Joha* became *Hodja*?

Presenter: **C   2   Listen and compare your ideas with this version.**

Jenny Ingram: Here is one of the Joha stories. It is called *Joha and the Donkey*.

One day, Joha took his son to the market in the next town. They only had one donkey. Joha walked and his son rode on the donkey. After a few miles, they walked past some people.
"Look at that young boy!" an old man said. "He has no respect for his father. He rides and his father walks!"
The boy felt very ashamed and said:
"Father, you must ride on the donkey and I will walk."
So Joha rode on the donkey and his son walked. After a few miles, they saw some more people.
"Look at that man!" a young boy said. "He has no feeling for his son. He rides and his son walks!"
Joha felt very ashamed and said:
"Son, we must both ride. Then no one can be angry with you or with me."
After a few miles, they went through a village.
"Look at those two people!" said a man with a donkey. "They have no feeling for their donkey. They are both riding the poor animal under this hot sun!"
"Son," said Joha. "We must carry the donkey. Then no one can be angry with us."
After a few miles, they came to the market. All the people started laughing:
"Look at those silly people. They are carrying a donkey. Why aren't they riding it?"

Presenter: **Theme 9: Sports and Leisure, Classifying Sports**
Lesson 1: Vocabulary
C   Listen to a paragraph. Then write one of the red or green words in each space. Change the form of the word if necessary.

Voice: There are many different kinds of sport. We play some sports with a ball – for example, football, tennis, rugby and golf. We play some sports with other players in a team. For example, football is a team sport.
Sometimes we need a piece of equipment to take part in a sport. We need a bicycle, of course, for cycling, and we need a stick for ice hockey.

Presenter: **Lesson 2: Listening**
B   1   Listen to the introduction. Write the missing words in *Categories* and *Definitions*.
Part 1.

Lecturer: Today I'm going to talk about sport. As you know, there are many different sports, but it is possible to classify them into three groups – classify is spelt C-L-A-S-S-I-F-Y. It comes from the word 'class'. Classifying means putting into groups. The first group contains racing sports – R-A-C-I-N-G – which means trying to go faster than another person. The second group of sports is opponent sports. An opponent – that's O-P-P-O-N-E-N-T – is someone you play against. Finally, there

are achievement sports. Achievement, of course, means reaching a certain level, a good level. Oh, sorry. Achievement is A-C-H-I-E-V-E-M-E-N-T. So, I'm going to classify sports into three groups and give examples of sports in each category or group.

Presenter: **B   2   Listen to Part 2. When the lecturer stops, guess the next word. Then listen and check.**
Part 2.

Lecturer: OK. So let's look at the first [PAUSE] group – racing. Trying to go faster than another [PAUSE] person. There are two sub-categories here. Sub means 'under'. So a sub-category is under a category. Some racing sports just use the power of the human [PAUSE] body. For example, running and [PAUSE] swimming. Other sports in this category use the power of [PAUSE] machines. Cycling uses [PAUSE] bicycles, motor racing uses [PAUSE] cars.
What about the second group – opponent sports? Once again, with opponent sports, there are two sub-[PAUSE] categories. The opponent might be a person or a [PAUSE] team. For example, we play tennis against one [PAUSE] person, but we play football against a [PAUSE] team.
Finally, there are achievement [PAUSE] sports. In achievement sports, there are also two [PAUSE] sub-categories. Sometimes we try to reach a target – T-A-R-G-E-T. For example, in golf, we try to get a white ball into a [PAUSE] hole. So that's a target [PAUSE] sport. Sometimes we try to achieve a particular quantity – distance, for example or [PAUSE] height. Quantity is Q-U-A-N-T-I-T-Y. In the long jump, we try to jump farther than all the other [PAUSE] people.

Presenter: **B   3   Listen to Part 2 again. Complete the *Sub-categories* section with headings under each arrow.**
[REPEAT OF LESSON 2 EXERCISE B2 WITHOUT PAUSES]

Presenter: **B   4   Listen to Part 2 again and write one example for each sub-category.**
[REPEAT OF LESSON 2 EXERCISE B3]

Presenter: **B   5   Listen to the summary of the lecture (Part 3) and check your answers.**
Part 3.

Lecturer: OK. So we have heard about three categories of sports – racing, opponent and achievement. We have seen that each category has two sub-categories. In racing it's human body and machine, in opponent sports it's person or team, and in achievement sports it's target or quantity. Before next time, can you think of ten sports and classify each one into one of the sub-categories from today's lecture?

Presenter: **D   2   Listen and check your answers.**

Voice:
against	column 6
ball	column 5
class	column 3
heard	column 7
quantity	column 4
racing	column 8
reach	column 1
target	column 3
team	column 1
that	column 2

Presenter: **Lesson 3: Learning new skills**
B Listen to Part 1 of the lecture from Lesson 2 again. Put your hand up when you hear an important word.
[REPEAT OF LESSON 2 EXERCISE B1]

Presenter: **C Listen to Part 2 of the lecture again. How does the lecturer show that these words are important? Tick one or more ways.**
[REPEAT OF LESSON 2 EXERCISE B3]

Presenter: **D 2 Listen and check your ideas.**
Voice:
so	column A
power	column A
opponent	column A
how	column B
know	column A
go	column A
also	column A
OK	column A

Presenter: **Lesson 4: Applying new skills**
B 2 Listen to the introduction. Listen for the important words. Correct Manuel's work below.
Part 1.
Lecturer: Today I'm going to talk about ball games. As you know, there are many different ball games, but it is possible to classify them into three groups. The first group contains games played mainly with the hands. The second group contains games played mainly with the feet. Finally, there are bat sports – sports played with some kind of bat, stick or racket. So, I'm going to classify sports into three groups and give examples of sports in each category or group.

Presenter: **C Listen to Part 2. When the lecturer stops, guess the next word. Then listen and check.**
Part 2.
Lecturer: OK. So let's look at the first [PAUSE] group. Hand sports. There are many hand sports, including basketball, rugby – that's R-U-G-B-Y, and of course, [PAUSE] handball.
What about the second [PAUSE] group? Sports played with the [PAUSE] feet. Actually, there is only one major sport in this [PAUSE] category. It's called football, of [PAUSE] course.
Finally, there are bat [PAUSE] sports. Sports played with a [PAUSE] bat. Of course, the bat has different [PAUSE] names in different sports. For example, in tennis the bat is called a [PAUSE] racket – R-A-C-K-E-T. The word comes from Arabic, 'rahat al yad', meaning the palm or inside of the [PAUSE] hand. In golf, it is called a [PAUSE] club – C-L-U-B. In ice hockey, it is called a [PAUSE] stick.

Presenter: **D Listen to Part 2 again.**
Part 2.
[REPEAT OF LESSON 4 EXERCISE C WITHOUT PAUSES]

Presenter: **E Listen to Part 3. Discuss in pairs.**
Part 3.
Lecturer: OK. So we have heard about three categories of ball games – hand sports, foot sports and bat sports. Why is it important to classify ball games? Because we must teach children to play at least one game in each category. This helps to develop their physical ability. Before next time, can you think of ten ball games or sports and classify each one into one of the categories from today's lecture?

Presenter: **Theme 10: Nutrition and Health, Nutrients and Food Groups**
Lesson 1: Vocabulary
B Listen to a paragraph. Then write one of the red or green words in each space.
Voice: Why do we eat? What a silly question! We eat because we are hungry. Well, that answer is true, in a way. But why do we feel hungry? We feel hungry because the body needs more energy. The whole body needs energy to move. Every part of the body needs energy to work correctly. We get energy from food. However, we have to be careful. If we don't use all the energy from food, the body keeps it. How does it keep it? It keeps it as fat. It is easy to use *new* energy from food. It is much harder to use the energy in fat. So, what's the answer? We must eat the right *amount* of food, and we must take exercise to use the extra energy. The food we normally eat is called our diet. Of course, we must eat the right kind of food as well. If we eat the right amount of the right *kind* of food, we will have a healthy diet. But what's the right *kind* of food? That's another question.

Presenter: **Lesson 2: Listening review (1)**
B Noura Hamed is studying Food Sciences at Greenhill College. She has a lecture today about food. Listen to the first part. When the lecturer stops, guess the next word. Did you guess correctly?
Male lecturer: Today I'm going to talk about food. Why does the human body need [PAUSE] food? Of course, the body needs food to [PAUSE] live. The body takes energy from [PAUSE] food. Energy is the ability to do [PAUSE] work. It also takes important [PAUSE] chemicals. Chemicals are things like calcium and magnesium. These chemicals help the parts of the body to work [PAUSE] correctly. We call the energy and chemicals in food [PAUSE] nutrients. As you probably know, there are several different types of [PAUSE] nutrient. The body needs different amounts of each [PAUSE] nutrient. If you have too much of a particular type, you can get [PAUSE] fat. If you have too little of a particular type, you can get [PAUSE] ill.

Presenter: **C 2 Listen to the first part again and check.**
[REPEAT OF LESSON 2 EXERCISE B WITHOUT PAUSES]

Presenter: **D Listen to the second part. What is the lecturer going to talk about this week? Tick one or more.**
Male lecturer: So, this week, I'm going to name the different nutrients. Then I'm going to give you some examples of foods that contain each type of nutrient. Next week, I'm going to talk about food groups and how much food you need from each group.

Presenter: **E 2 Listen to the third part and complete the names of the nutrients.**
Male lecturer: OK. First, what are the different nutrients? There are five main types. Firstly, there are carbohydrates. Secondly, there is protein. We spell that P-R-O-T-E-I-N. That's E-I-N, not I-E-N. Thirdly, we have vitamins – V-I-T-A-M-I-N-S. Fourthly, there are fats. Meat and fish contain fats. Finally, there are minerals – M-I-N-E-R-A-L-S.

Presenter:	**E 4 Listen to the fourth part. Check and complete the table.**
Male lecturer:	Where do we find the main nutrients? We find carbohydrates in food like bread, pasta and rice. There is protein in meat and fish. There is also protein in cheese. What about vitamins? Fruit, like apples and oranges, contains vitamins. So do vegetables like carrots and peas. Next, fats. Meat and fish contain fats. There are also fats in products like milk and cheese. Finally, there are minerals. We find minerals in many foods, but particularly in milk, meat and eggs.
Presenter:	**F Listen to the fifth part. What does the lecturer want you to do before next week?**
Male lecturer:	OK. So, we have looked at nutrients and foods that contain them. Next week, food groups and how much food you need from each group. Before next week, could you look up food groups on the Internet and make some notes of different ideas about them? OK? So I want you to do some research on food groups on the Internet and note some things down.
Presenter:	**Lesson 3: Listening review (2)** **A 2 Listen and check your ideas.**
Male lecturer:	Today I'm going to talk about food. Why does the human body need food? Of course, the body needs food to live. The body takes energy from food. Energy is the ability to do work. It also takes important chemicals. Chemicals are things like calcium and magnesium. These chemicals help the parts of the body to work correctly. We call the energy and chemicals in food nutrients. As you probably know, there are several different types of nutrient. The body needs different amounts of each nutrient. If you have too much of a particular type, you can get fat. If you have too little of a particular type, you can get ill. So, this week, I'm going to name the different nutrients. Then I'm going to give you some examples of foods that contain each type of nutrient. Next week, I'm going to talk about food groups and how much food you need from each group. Where do we find the main nutrients? We find carbohydrates in food like bread, pasta and rice. There is protein in meat and fish. There is also protein in cheese. What about vitamins? Fruit, like apples and oranges, contains vitamins. So do vegetables like carrots and peas. Next, fats. Meat and fish contain fats. There are also fats in products like milk and cheese. Finally, there are minerals. We find minerals in many foods, but particularly in milk, meat and eggs. OK. So, we have looked at nutrients and foods that contain them. Next week, food groups and how much food you need from each group. Before next week, could you look up food groups on the Internet and make some notes of different ideas about them? OK? So I want you to do some research on food groups on the Internet and note some things down.
Presenter:	**C 2 Listen and check your ideas.**
Voice:	a talk work course call b type rice give finally c main contain have take d so know does note e meat cheese bread protein f nutrient fruit much food g about amount how group

Presenter:	**D 1 Listen to the spelling of more words from the lecture. Write the letters.**
Voice:	H-U-M-A-N N-U-T-R-I-E-N-T C-H-E-M-I-C-A-L-S O-R-A-N-G-E C-A-R-R-O-T P-A-S-T-A B-O-D-Y F-I-N-A-L-L-Y E-N-E-R-G-Y
Presenter:	**E 1 Listen again to part of the lecture. Which words does the lecturer define?**
Male lecturer:	Today I'm going to talk about food. Why does the human body need food? Of course, the body needs food to live. The body takes energy from food. Energy is the ability to do work. It also takes important chemicals. Chemicals are things like calcium and magnesium. These chemicals help the parts of the body to work correctly. We call the energy and chemicals in food nutrients. As you probably know, there are several different types of nutrient. The body needs different amounts of each nutrient. If you have too much of a particular type, you can get fat. If you have too little of a particular type, you can get ill.
Presenter:	**E 2 Listen again. Make notes of the definition of each word.** [REPEAT OF LESSON 3 EXERCISE E1]
Presenter:	**F 2 Listen and check your ideas.**
Male lecturer:	We call the energy and chemicals in food nutrients. As you probably know, there are several different types of nutrient. The body needs different amounts of each nutrient. If you have too much of a particular type, you can get fat. If you have too little of a particular type, you can get ill.
Presenter:	**Lesson 4: Listening review (3)** **B Noura has another lecture on her Food Sciences course. Listen to the first part. When the lecturer stops, guess the next word. Did you guess correctly?**
Male lecturer:	Last week I talked about nutrients in [PAUSE] food. I explained that there are five main [PAUSE] nutrients. The main nutrients, if you remember, are carbohydrates, protein, vitamins, fats and [PAUSE] minerals. This week I'm going to talk about food groups and healthy [PAUSE] eating. So, first. What are food [PAUSE] groups? Well, you can probably work it out from the [PAUSE] name. A food group is, simply, a group of [PAUSE] foods. There are six main food [PAUSE] groups. Some have the same name as the nutrients that they [PAUSE] contain. But some are [PAUSE] different. So first I'm going to tell you the six main food [PAUSE] groups. Then I'm going to talk about putting these groups together in a healthy [PAUSE] way. Finally, I'm going to ask you to think about your own [PAUSE] diet.
Presenter:	**C 2 Listen to the first part again and check.** [REPEAT OF LESSON 4 EXERCISE B WITHOUT PAUSES]

Presenter: **D 2 Listen to the second part and check your ideas.**

Male
lecturer: The six main food groups are as follows:
Number 1: fats; Number 2: carbohydrates – they're nutrients, of course; then 3 – vegetables; 4 – fruit; 5 – dairy products; and 6 – meat and fish.
One food group may need some explanation. What are dairy products? They are mainly milk and the products from milk – in other words, butter and cheese. English-speakers usually include eggs in dairy products, too.

Presenter: **E 2 Listen to the third part and check your ideas.**

Male
lecturer: OK. So what is the connection between the six food groups and healthy eating? Scientists say that a healthy diet consists of the correct balance between the foods in the different groups. But what is the correct balance? There is quite a lot of argument about this. I'm going to give you one idea. It comes from American scientists.
In the USA, food scientists have made a pyramid of the food groups. This pyramid shows the balance between the different groups. Fats are at the top of the pyramid. According to the American scientists, we should only have one portion of fats each day. At the next level of the pyramid, we have dairy products on one side and meat and fish on the other. The American scientists recommend three portions of dairy products and two portions of meat or fish each day. At the third level, there are vegetables on one side and fruit on the other. Apparently we should have four portions of fruit and three portions of vegetables. Finally, at the bottom of the pyramid there are the carbohydrates. The scientists say we should eat ten portions of carbohydrates.

Presenter: **E 3 Listen to the third part again and complete the figure. Copy the spelling of the words from Exercise A. Shade or colour in the squares.**
[REPEAT OF LESSON 4 EXERCISE E2]

Presenter: **F Listen to the last part of the lecture. What does the lecturer want you to do?**

Male
lecturer: Finally, today – what about your diet? Is it balanced? Think about a normal day. Do you have ten portions of carbohydrates – that's pieces of bread, pasta, rice, potatoes – not chips, of course, because they have fat on them? Do you have four portions of vegetables? Make a list of the foods you eat on an average day. Put the foods into the six main food groups. Work out a diet pyramid for you. Is it balanced? Is it top-heavy? Or does it stick out in the middle? We'll look at some of your food pyramids next time.